NIGGERS GO HOME

BLACK LIFE IN AMERICA

WHY DO THEY
HATE US
SO MUCH?

NIGGERS GO HOME

BLACK LIFE IN AMERICA

Michael Melancon

Printed by DiggyPOD, Inc., in the United States of America
First Printing, 2020

M. Melancon

ISBN: 978-1-7362172-2-1

TABLE OF CONTENTS

INTRODUCTION

I chose to write this memoir due to my need for self expression, as well as reflection as a Black American. As a subject of many countless racial and discriminatory issues and experiences relating to continued societal oppression, discrimination, and racism, I feel that writing about my personal experiences is a way for self-healing and to give myself a sense of "freedom", freedom of speech and the freedom to express myself without fear. A feeling of, in some way, control of my own destiny.

The main goal in writing this book was to tell and share my experiences. Not only do I share my experiences, I realize I have unintentionally offered a bit of education as well regarding America's race relations. I share not only my own experiences but examples of racist conflicts and attacks experienced by other non-black minorities subjected at the hands of America's racists. In this memoir of racists experiences, I felt compelled to support these experiences through research of other historical and current events that have made its way into American literature, such as histori-cal documents, books, periodicals, daily news broadcasts and social media in order to show and prove a commonality of American culture in relation to racism. With all of the cur-rent and overtly racial issues that have been emerging and resurfacing in ways not seen since the Civil Rights era of the 1960s, I kept hearing a common and growing noise; the ever-increasing noise of racist attitudes and views conscious and unconscious. To the unconscious outsider to racial in-justice, who often doubt or even believe that racism exists, I want to educate those people about what it is like to grow up and live in their same America, but through the eyes of a Black American. I want to share a common experience with other Black Americans and other minority groups who experience racism in America.

Through the racism I experienced, from as early as I can recall from my first childhood experiences to the present, I intend to inform the non-black reader, the reader who hon-estly and innocently believes that racism does not exist, that systemic racism does exist. In spite of the fact that some people have not had any personal experiences with racism or have never witnessed any incidents of racism, accounts of these experiences by those that have presented factual claims should not be excused, ignored or denied as having occurred. The black community's reactions following the murder of George Floyd (and almost 30 years prior with the beating of

Rodney King) is a reaction to the direct experience of racism and terrorism that Black Americans have been dealing with their entire lives. This everyday experience happens when we leave our homes to go to school, to go shopping, to go to work, in the courts, on public transportation, and anywhere and everywhere in American society. Black Americans will face racism and bigotry. The day-to-day stress of being subjugated to racist events and racist environments leaves Black Americans full of stress and anxiety. This has played a part in my daily life way too often!

The acknowledgment and self-awareness of our personal experiences with racism are not false claims, false perceptions or misunderstandings, as some other non-blacks and even some blacks would have you believe. Black Americans are often accused of "pulling the race card" when they feel they have been the subject of some form of unjust treatment by other non- blacks. In some rare instances, I have seen that to be true, but in more instances, this has become a way of life. When Black Americans legitimately express their experiences of racism, it's usually with other Black Americans who understand and can empathize with one another. When these experiences are shared with other non-blacks it is an attempt to get others to understand our experiences. Protests, marches, and riots are the explosive results of the daily bombardment of collectively simmering racist assaults on Black Americans generation after generation.

I was prompted to write this book now rather than later as a result of the countless movements and protests in America after the tragic death of George Floyd. Although the idea of writing this book came to me years ago, long before the death of Mr. Floyd, I had planned on writing it once I retired. However, with retirement on the horizon, I felt that I could no longer delay the recollection of my experiences. With the continuous racism, discrimination, and harassment I have been bombarded with and experienced throughout my life as a Black American, I decided that I could no longer wait and that I needed to start writing immediately. I felt that now is the time to begin this journey of sharing my experiences as a citizen of the United States of America. I started writing this book in June 2020, and while I was writing it, America was in a deep crisis. A viral health crisis is affecting the entire globe and has significantly changed the way we live our lives and the virus of racism in America, which has taken on a turbulent and monumental movement throughout the country. It has also spilled over into many other countries. Although racism is no new phenomenon in America, it appears to have laid dormant in terms of its overt reflections and display of the nation's bigots. Thanks to new media technology, racists activities, racists attacks and racist supporters have made their way onto America's main stage, with media coverage and many new internet platforms have the goal of spreading more hate and dividing a multicultural America. The daily bombardment of both viruses has left this country weary and very divided. With a lack of leadership in the White House, doomsday appears not to be too far away! When I began writing this book, the interruption of "Breaking News" stories and Facebook posts on the topic of racism was quite overwhelming. Combined with the worldwide virus, this is a lot to say the least. The daily racist news has played right into my drive to tell my story sooner than later. As I mentioned before, this book wasn't due to commence until after I retire in mid-2021, but the effect of these two viruses has prompted me and moved me to go beyond my daily routine of work, exercise, and studies.

In this book I recount numerous interactions with racism that I have had throughout my life, from citizens to teachers to police and everything else in between. Unfortunately, many encounters that I had with the police were undoubtedly racially motivated. Thankfully, my experiences were not physically abusive or violent as we see in many other cases. These recounts are in no way meant to bash the police as a whole. It's merely a true story of my life living as a black child and adult in American society. After all that has been going on in recent times regarding American policing, I do not believe that defunding police departments is the solution to bad policing, as what has been called for by many activists throughout the nation. Law enforcement officials face a very challenging and tough job and not everyone can do the job. It takes courage, bravery, sincerity, and care for the WHOLE community in order to be a respected and dignified law enforcement professional. The job is even more difficult when working in a community where there are cultural differences and ethnic diversity, which are not familiar to many of the police men and women who are assigned and tasked to work in these diverse and minority communities. Much respect and appreciation go towards those police departments and officers who take the time to understand and recognize those differences and who have taken the oath to "serve and protect" ALL CITIZENS they serve. I have come across law enforcement professionals who are true professionals, and it is my belief that the majority of law enforcement professionals outnumber those that are racists and, by far, deemed unprofessional. But I do believe there needs to be a major overhaul in policing throughout this country. With reflections of my life as a Black American youth and adult, I would have to say that at least 80% of the police contacts I had were unpleasant and unprofessional, to say the least. Although I believe that most police are truly professional, my encounters as a Black American civilian were unpleasant.

As a Black American civilian, you are a target of racial profiling, which most commonly seems to occur when you are "driving while black". Time and time again, especially as a youth, you experience that same anxiety-producing traffic stop. The police see you, and if they're traveling in the opposite direction, they make that quick U-turn, get up on your rear bumper and follow you while running your plates. In my situations, and although they never found anything wrong after running my plates, they still would pull me over anyways. Not because I committed a traffic violation or had a warrant, but to interrogate, harass, and intimidate. These types of encounters and experiences as a Black American have been common practice on how police treat and interact with dark-skinned people. This is what we have seen historically and what is currently taking place. Ultimately, this direct proof of experiences shared by many people of color demands a major shift in policing all-across America.

My book is written to help educate and bring awareness to the issues of being black in America. Although I anticipate and hope that many Black Americans will read and support this book and will be able to relate to my experiences, my target audience are all other minorities and empathetic White Americans who are not aware of racism and/or systemic racism. Not only do I want to help educate and bring awareness to what I and other Black Americans experience and endure in this country, I am also writing this book as a symbol of peace and racial tolerance for ALL, to bring this country together for a true UNITED States of America. The citizens in the United States today are no longer just Black and White. Citizens come from many, many different ethnic and cultural backgrounds. For those that read this book, imagine what it would be like if all cultures united and gave way to respect one another. Although America is known as the United States, the word "united" has only meant that the 50 states of America share a commonality, not as people, but politically and economically. However, as a people and citizens of this country, there has never been total unity, and there is no "united" regarding the citizens. We are living in a time where the United States of America can no longer be culturally and ethnically self-absorbed, self-reflected, segregated and concerned only about one's own identity and background. Continuous division equals the ultimate demise and collapse of the greater social structure meant to be united. As human beings, we are ONE, and should not be divided by race but related as humans. If America is to become a healthier environment for all, then there needs to be systematic changes that are inclusive to all.

Making America Great (which has never been true) for the first time will require an all-one-nation attitude amongst all citizens, as the great nation it was meant to be. We cannot afford to be divided and further pitted against one another. It's truly bad business for the country. The uniqueness of ethnic diversity in this country offers a wealth of learning and creativity. It's amazing that we can live in a country and have so many different peoples and we can share life experiences side-by-side. It's a travesty, however, that we take this unique opportunity for granted. Rather than building walls to keep others out, Americans of all backgrounds should be extending open arms and sharing their culture. American culture is made up of many cultures that desperately need to be shared, tolerated, and accepted. We should be celebrating everyone's culture! The United States of America should be leading the world in setting the example of what it should look like to be civil humans, as the United States is a representation of all ethnic backgrounds across the world!

BLACK AMERICAN VS. "AFRICAN-AMERICAN"

Throughout this book, you will notice I use the term "Black" to refer to Americans of African descent, those who are the descendants of the first African slaves in America. Some prefer to use "African-American," but that term, to me, gives a false sense of the true meaning of the Black American, of which I have never felt comfortable. I prefer to refer to myself and others like me as Black Americans, although somewhat crude sounding. Some will say the word black denotes no significant value as if compared to a color crayon and/or directly related to the term "Negro," which has since been considered offensive. "The word "Negro," or "nigger," is a white man's word to make us feel inferior. If men despise Negroes, they will not despise them less if Negroes are called "colored" or "Afro-American." (DuBois, 1928). Black Americans continue to struggle with the proper and politically correct words used to identify us as a people, which has been historically controversial and a constant struggle for a rootless people in search of meaning, culture, and identity. In 1988, the term African-American officially became the term identifier for the Black American. This official recognition was headed by prominent Black American leaders such as Jesse Jackson. "To being called African American has cultural integrity," Jackson said. "It puts us in our proper historical context. Every ethnic group in this country has a reference to some land base. Some historical cultural base. African-Americans have hit their level of cultural maturity. There are Armenian-Americans and Jewish-Americans and Arab-Americans and Italian-Americans. And with a degree of accepted and reasonable pride, they connect their heritage to their mother country and where they are now." (Martin, 1991). Although I respect and appreciate Jesse Jackson and his movement for a more acceptable and respectable term for Black Americans, I disagree. Creating names, changing names, seeking alternative descriptions of a group of people will not create cultural integrity. Integrity comes from one's inner-self, which is on constant display to those in observance. The judgment of character rather than the judgment of a name change is the basis of integrity. However, within any culture or group, you will have those individuals with great integrity and those with less. The Black American has had his roots and culture eradicated by involuntary oppression, leaving us with little to no recollection of culture related to the motherland. Therefore, the Black American culture is always shifting, is always fluid, is always reinventing, is always creative, and, more importantly, is always flexible, which derives itself from the experiences of life here in America. All other ethnic minorities have direct ties and intact cultures of music, food, and language tracing back to countries outside of America. Black Americans do not.

Although it is suggested that racist whites were using the term "Negro" to identify blacks in much more of a negative and inferior way, the term "Negro" was being used long before that, before Africans were taken to be used as slaves. The term was not used in an inferior way, but rather as a description of darker-skinned people and used interchangeably with the Moors of Africa, a very dark-skinned group of people. The term "Negro" came from the Portuguese and Spanish dating back to the mid-16th century, commonly used to describe people from Africa and Australia. The English also referred to Africans as Negros prior to slavery and during the mid-1500s they were trading with Africans on the African coast.

To me, Black represents pride and perseverance, strength and resilience, boldness and beauty, sacrifice and achievement, which is in direct contrast to the term "Negro" used and adopted by slave owners and racists whites in America. "I'm Black and I'm proud" has been my personal and inspirational slogan playing in my head through my college years and adult life as I deal with day-to-day racism. It is one of the tools that I use to help keep me focused and positive despite the overarching effects of systemic racism. I thank James Brown, the Godfather of Soul, who in 1968 came out with the song, "Say It Loud, I'm Black and I'm Proud". Growing up and listening to the song made my soul lift every time I heard it playing on the radio or on my parents' record player! To me, as a Black American, this is culture. Black American culture, along with many other great and positive Black American songwriters, musicians, and artists, is what makes you feel connected in a world that offers little significance to your ethnic identity. This culture in music was not born in Africa, it was born right here in America.

Furthermore, to me African American implies that there is a solid connection, a solid foundation that ties us Black Americans to the continent of Africa and that there was some legal systematic process and procedure that the "African- American" went through for obtaining American citizenship. When you reference any other Americans (such as in the example noted by Jesse Jackson) whose ethnicities are Mexican, Chinese, Indian, and so on, you refer to these groups of people as Mexican-American, Chinese-American, Indian-American and so on and so forth. These groups of people, whether themselves or their first-generation parents, grandparents, or great grandparents, all went through a formalized process to become American Citizens, which is in direct contrast to the reality of the Black American's existence in America. What all of the other ethnic groups have in common is an intact culture, an intact heritage, and an intact language directly related to a history of culture outside of America, their homeland. And I must take this moment to speak to those minorities who have this intact culture. It is a shame that there are those ethnic American minorities who are more concerned with and choose to assimilate with white America at the cost of their own cultural backgrounds and identity, which I have to say is a travesty! Embrace the positive aspects of your heritage, your culture, and your rich traditions. Remember Africans in America were forced to forget their history through family separation, torture, and death! I say treasure your history that was passed down from generation to generation and never forget where your people came from. Make sure your offspring learn the language of your ancestors. Do not take your culture for granted! Black Americans are the only group of ethnic minorities in America whose culture was eradicated and lost forever. From the time Africans were brought to America as slaves in the early 1600s, and remained slaves through the 1800s. That's over 200 years of captivity and bondage!

During those slave days, the white slave owners and traders continuously broke up families and bred slaves like animals. These slave masters stripped Africans of their native languages, their native culture, their native ways of life. They made slaves change their names to European names. The list goes on and on. Here's a truth: "African-Americans have been free in this country for less time than they were enslaved. Blacks have been free for 152 years, which means that most Americans are only two to three generations away from slavery." (Douez & Costello, 2017). It was 1619 when the first Africans arrived in America as slaves, and hundreds of years later, in 1863, America's President Lincoln abolished slavery. However, that did not go into effect until 1865. 246 years of slavery and 401 years later, who are we? WHO ARE WE? Our ancestors were enslaved longer than we have been free! We know our people originated from Africa, but truly, who are we? Many of my Asian and Mexican brothers and sisters can tell you, "Oh, I am going back to visit my grandparents and cousins in Mexico," or "I am going to the Philippines to visit with my uncles and aunts for the holidays". Black Americans cannot do that. We can't say we are going back to the motherland to visit family members. If any of us do go back to Africa, it's most likely as a tourist or missionary visit, but not to visit family members. We were stripped of our identity and made to forget who we are.

My next-door neighbor, a tall, thin, and very dark-skinned man named Mwengu Siwiti, speaks with a very thick and heavy native African tongue. He often speaks of family back in Zambia, Africa where he grew up. He talks about life with his eight siblings and being raised by his grandmother in the village. He recalls hunting, coming across lions and adds that he moved away from the village and his grandmother when he was around 10 years of age to rejoin his parents and other siblings in a city in Tanzania. It was there that he would attend school for the first time. Due to his age, he was thrust into the fifth grade where he had to catch on really quick and catch-up to his grade level. He recalls this time in his life being very difficult. Impressed by my neighbor who speaks five different languages and has obtained two Master's Degrees, one in Engineering, it's made me reflect on life as a Black American. Although I set goals and have made several successful accomplishments in my own life, it is truly humbling that this man whose roots come from a tribe in Africa (where there are over 72 different language dialects from his province of Zambia) has made such accomplishments here in America. When he came to America decades ago, he too, like many other immigrants, went through the process of becoming an American citizen. With his ties to his home-land, his African language, his speaking of the African dishes and foods from Zambia, the dress and the culture, is the direct lineage of what it means to me to be an African. He further mentions that he is the President of a local Zambia club here in Sacramento, where they get together for festivals and activities. To me, this is a true reflection of what an African- American is, one who has knowledge and memory of his homeland in which he often travels back to visit relatives. Because Black Americans do not share these same experiences as Mr. Siwiti, or have specific knowledge of their African ancestors, Black Americans can only assume what part of the vast continent of Africa their ancestors truly came from. Even if Black Americans know their specific origins in Africa, there is no language, no name, no recognizable family members such as cousins, aunts, and uncles. Black Americans are like the "lost and found" in an American school cafeteria or like the "foster-kids" of a nation. After all the contributions and labor of African slaves and freed Blacks, who significantly paid their dues and gave their lives to build America, we deserve the right to be titled "American". Not "African-American," but "American". I speculate that this might likely be too confusing and controversial for America as a whole, so I prefer Black American, and it's what I will be using throughout this book.

BACKGROUND

In 1971 I was the first born of two brothers of an intact family in San Francisco, California. My parents at the time were living in the Fillmore district, a predominantly black neighborhood during the 70s and 80s. By the time I reached my first year of life, our family had moved South and settled into the city of South San Francisco. When my youngest brother was born nine years later, and not less than a year later, my mother and father would be divorced, and my mother was left to raise the three of us until my step-father joined us in 1988. In my first decade of life, I was innocently exposed to the phrase "Niggers Go Home" (NGH). I will be referencing this abbreviation frequently throughout my writings, which from time to time will be more of an abstract view of a true meaning, delicately used to compliment the instigator's bottom-line meaning of a wish for an extinct group, the Black American. Through self-reflection, Black Americans living in a racist society acknowledge that their lives do not matter under a historically oppressive regime. Although this word is one of the most disrespectful and hateful words you can use when referring to a Black American, it is my raw truth, my experience, and my exposure to racism and hate in America. During the mid-70s and through the 80s, I would encounter this phrase with great frequency. In the early 90s, I moved to Sacramento to get away from the routine and eventually ended up getting my Bachelor's degree in Social Work from California State University, Sacramento. While living in Sacramento, I experienced more racism, which made it a bit more challenging and difficult to navigate my way through life as I pushed towards my goals and success.

THE NEIGHBORHOOD AND GRADE SCHOOL

I grew up in the Westborough neighborhood of South San Francisco. It was diverse during that time, but the majority of families were white. Many black families during the 70s and early 80s were settling in this town, and the black presence (including other minorities such as Filipinos and Indians) was growing. The word around town during those days was that whites were moving out far north and east, as too many blacks were moving in. A couple of my white friends and their families headed north, including a white neighbor who would eventually find his way to Idaho, which is not known for being a very ethnically diverse state.

In 1958, a poll was taken by whites which reported that 44 percent of whites said they would move if a black family became their next-door neighbor. (Thernstrom, 1998). I would imagine this being the reason for whites moving out and heading north during my years growing up in the neighborhood. While researching this phenomenon of whites moving out as a result of Black Americans moving in, I came across a term that I have never heard of from Wikipedia. "White flight" or "white exodus" means "the sudden or gradual large-scale migration of white people from areas becoming more racially or ethnoculturally diverse." My observations were no longer just gossip, but were exposed as truths as noted in many periodicals. The black families in Westborough found their way in this diverse community. Most families knew one another and many had developed social networks such as the Black Unity Council. They often helped each other out with things like child-care, fundraising, and community activities and picnics.

As I entered the public elementary school system, I became keenly aware that something was odd about me. I could not really put my finger on it at the time other than recalling specific incidents starting as early as my preschool year. There are not many things that stand out to me or that I remember in preschool, but something left me feeling humiliated and shameful at the young age of four or five and this would be my first experience of what I now know as racism. This first experience of a racist attack was something that I couldn't understand until much later in life. A friend of mine once told me, "It's not always about what a person does to you, but about how that person made you feel." This will forever be stained in my mind. It was the first time I'd be disciplined by someone other than my father or a family member. The schools that I went to had predominantly white teachers, except an occasional summer school stint in the Fillmore district back in San Francisco where most teachers and students were all black. Most of the white teachers in South San Francisco I was exposed to had some sort of dislike for me. Some more than others. Let's just say too many times I was left feeling shame and worthless.

Preschool is where my first encounter or recollection with racism would occur. I had been placed in the corner of the classroom, made to face the wall. Prior to that, I received several smacks to the hand with a ruler by the white teacher. I questioned myself. What did I do to deserve this, what did I do wrong? Initially I had no clue. That same question I would be asking myself years later (What did I do?) after many encounters with the police. "Why?" I asked. The only thing I concluded at the time was the expression that I made as the teacher was reading a book during circle time. It was a picture book and the next page the teacher turned to was a picture of a snake. Well, I hated snakes! I had nightmares of snakes! So, I stuck my tongue out in reaction to my dislike for snakes and I can only imagine how my face must have looked! Without me saying a word, and without any explanation from the teacher of what was going on or what I did, I was told to get up from the circle and come up to the front of the classroom. The teacher then asked for my left hand while I stood in front of the other students. She commenced smacking it with a ruler at least three to four times and then told me to go to the corner of the classroom to sit on a stool wearing a dunce hat. How humiliated I felt! Many of you who are not familiar with what a dunce hat is, it is a hat in the shape of a cone that was worn on top of your head while sitting in the corner.

This was a punishment tool used by teachers for misbehaving children as a form of humiliation. Several sources say the dunce hat was used in the 50s and 60s and had been banned, but I was in preschool in the 70s, so apparently, it was still being used. At such a young age, this would become one of the most highlighted moments of my life during that time. More so because I had never been disciplined by a non-family member and I was clueless as to the reason for the punishment. Which leads me into another incident where I was punished in school and didn't know what I had done wrong.

I believe I must have been in the third or fourth grade. I was actually on a school break, perhaps spring break. My cousin, who lived in the Oakland area at the time and was going to a catholic private school in Berkeley, was not on break yet. Since I spent many weekends and summers with my cousin, I went and spent a day with him at his school where I was able to attend class, go to lunch, and play on the playground during recess as a guest. I will never forget this time. We brought one of our favorite candies to school,

"Rolos." I was excited and delighted to be at school with my cousin, who is more like a brother to me. I couldn't wait for recess time. As soon as we were out on the playground enjoying the warm sun, the kids started a game of tag. Not more than five minutes into it, I was being chased down by yard-duty with a whistle blaring. My thoughts were that yard-duty must be after someone else, I'm not even from this school and no one knows me. Not to mention I know I did nothing wrong. But sure enough, it was me that yard-duty was after. As she sternly pointed her finger and blew her whistle at me, she motioned to me to come over to her. As I hesitantly approached her, she instructed me to sit on the bench for the rest of the recess. As I asked how come, I was told that I was in trouble, and that was it. I am thinking, oh damn, I'm in trouble. How will I explain this to my aunt and uncle, yet worse, to my father, of whom I was deathly afraid? My world felt as though it was coming to an end. But I was never given an explanation as to why I was in trouble, nor did it ever get reported to my aunt and uncle. Looking back, maybe I was running too fast as a black boy in a catholic school! You know these catholic schools often have strange rules. My first year in high school in San Francisco had a very strange rule, but that's a topic for a whole other conversation. Anyways, I am confident that my punishment must have had something to do with my black face.

My first and second-grade teachers were different though. They were nice white ladies that seemed to be caring and fair from what I recall. But the third through fifth-grade teachers, oh wow! I would say a parent of any race would be concerned with the menacing looks and harassing demeanor they gave to me and other black students. However, I never told my parents what I was going through or experiencing. I have always been the type to deal with my issues within. At the time, I guess I really did not understand it anyways. Honestly, I thought it was just me. My fourth-grade teacher seemed to be one of the worst. Heller, I think was her last name. I recall often being ridiculed for everything. I was extremely quiet throughout grade school, trying not to be noticed by the teachers. I wanted to join the band and I wanted to learn how to play the saxophone in the fourth grade, but I was told my fingers were too little. I was told to play the clarinet. Whether it was true or not that my fingers were too small, I just recalled feeling like shit. Who the fuck wanted to play the clarinet? But because I wanted to play music so bad, I ended up taking on the clarinet and actually enjoying it! But as far as the school band and instruments go, my preference was either the drums or saxophone. I was intrigued by the way my elementary school friend Brian played the drums. He seemed to me to be much better than Sheila E! Needless to say, I wanted to try playing the drums myself. I had convinced my mom into getting me a drum set for Christmas, but it was in no way comparable to that of Brian's drum set. I think this drum set may have been from Toys R Us. Just so you know, my new drum set didn't survive Christmas evening!

I recall my fifth-grade teacher poking fun at the size of my butt, asking why it was so big and pointing fun at me after showing up to school on crutches after a weekend mishap at home. Was this normal coming from an adult teacher? I guess I thought it was for me. Although my sixth-grade teacher seemed a bit more pleasant, I recall her little game of trying to catch me off guard as often as she could. She would have the whole class take turns reading from our textbooks. She would randomly call on us to read aloud. I noticed that she would watch me a lot, frequently peering above the frame of her reading glasses. If I appeared distracted, she would immediately call on me. If I read a word wrong or lost my place, she would scorn me in front of the class.

Other than being on edge and anxious about being caught off guard, I did muster up the cognitive ability to pay attention in class despite all that (not letting white educators convince my mother that I was special needs or needed ADD or ADHD meds). Learning for me was a bore in elementary school. I can say I pretty much hated school, especially when having to deal with the teachers. When it came to learning I did enjoy history, but I had issues with history, such as not seeing much in regards to Black Americans and their depiction in America. On very, very rare occasions outside of Columbus, friendly Pilgrims and contented Native Americans stories, the subject of slavery was briefly mentioned if even mentioned at all, which to me seemed more like a fictional tale rather than an actual event in time. The whole time in grade school, all you learned about was how great white people were; Benjamin Franklin, George Washington, Andrew Jackson, the Wright Brothers, and so on. This was fine to me, but I questioned if there was anything Black Americans did that was great too! After public school, in college and through my own research, I would learn that indeed there were many, many Black Americans that did many great things and made great contributions to America. Do you ever think and wonder how vehicle traffic in America seems to run in such an orderly way and fashion compared to other underdeveloped countries? Thanks to a fine Black American by the name of Garrett Morgan, who in 1916 developed the traffic light signal. Madam C.J. Walker, born in 1867, became the first self-made female millionaire in America from developing hair care products and cosmetics for black women. George Washington Carver invented peanut butter. In more recent times, in 1990 a NASA scientist by the name of Lonnie Johnson invented the super soaker water gun. However, the depiction of Black Americans in the public-school system was of sad, poor-looking blacks in some type of scenario as a servant. But we were taught how great the Pilgrims were and how they conducted "fair" trade with the "Indians". So, you sit there in class, you see black people of earlier times and you realize the whole class is looking at the images of poor black servants, people who look like me! Comparing these images to the images of successful, well-dressed and healthy-looking whites, you unconsciously begin to feel quite inferior when comparing yourself to the white race. From that point on, you begin to realize that as a Black American, you do not matter. You feel that your race is just merely in existence and are only tolerated in order to serve white people. That is what I got out of elementary school history. However, the only black history with some sort of positivity and a bit of significance (which was not instructed in depth or given great meaning) was that of Martin Luther King Junior. Thank God for that!

Racist views and attitudes in school not only came from the teachers, but from the white kids as well. Outside of the classroom and on the playground, I learned terms such as "wet-back," "beaners," "chinks," "gooks," and "ching-chongs". Not to mention the insulting noises they made as they mocked Asian language while pulling their eyes back into a slant. During my elementary school years and on the playground, this is where I first learned and heard of such derogatory terms used to refer to other non-black minorities.

As I reflect on my elementary school experiences, I recall losing focus periodically. Like I said, I hated school. Any chance I got, I would go to the office "feeling sick". Did I actually feel sick during those years or was I looking for an escape? I think perhaps it was both. I felt sick because of the overwhelming anxiety flowing through my body and was looking for an escape in order to avoid another day of possible humiliation. Although I thought it was just me, in the sixth grade, I noticed that my black friend who sat on the opposite side of the classroom was also being treated quite similarly. As I thought about my "place" in grade school, I began to realize it wasn't my place to be there, but I was required to go. While entering the sixth grade, I recall my little brother entering the first grade. I remember thinking, would he go through all that I went through in this public-school? "The unfortunate reality is that Black Americans experience subtle and overt discrimination from preschool all the way to college. Black boys are almost three times as likely to be suspended than white boys and black girls are four times as likely to be suspended than white girls." (Douez & Costello, 2017). Would my brother face the same humiliation? I was concerned about him! Needless to say, my mother eventually pulled him from the school I had gone to and sent him to another school nearby. My brother was way more expressive than I was and I'm sure my mom figured out that something was very wrong with that school. Recently, another black friend of mine commented on his elementary school experience and related that at the same school I went to, he had faced the same humiliation. However, he did end up going to the other local school in hopes of better treatment.

While in grade school, I was fond of fast muscle cars, and I always knew that I wanted to be a stunt car driver. I think it was either in the fifth or sixth grade, I remember taking some sort of test, somewhat like a survey test. This test was supposed to give you an inclination on what you might want to do as a career or become as an adult. I was never so disappointed in my life! I could have sworn all my answers to this survey test would have concluded that I was destined to be some Hollywood stunt car driver! Mind you, the numerous occupations they had listed as possible careers included stunt car driver. Some of my friends will tell you that Hollywood stunt car drivers would not have anything on me. Not a chance. This damn test said I would most likely be a bus driver or sanitation driver. No disrespect to all the sanitation and bus drivers, but hell no! That did not seem exciting at all! How the hell am I going to jump a bus or get sideways (drifting-making the rear of your car skid to the left or right while driving) in a sanitation truck! I mean, I am sure I could have, but I am sure that would have come with a huge cost and not in my favor! So just like the saxophone dream, my dreams of becoming a stunt car driver slipped away. I always wondered in the later years to come,

was that test racially biased or motivated? I am sure I bub-
bled in my response to the test as being a Black American,
you know, the same shit you see on applications everywhere
you turn. If America wasn't a racist society, then why would
you need to have folks identify their racial identities?

As I moved onto middle school, the environment took
on a totally different form. Although most of the teachers
were white, the teachers seemed much nicer and the school
made you feel like you were growing up and becoming
somewhat independent. In middle school, I do not recall
hearing or seeing much of any racial issues. Middle school
was the best experience I had in the public-school system.
All of the races seemed to get along and seemed to be inclusive of one another. I didn't hear the racial slurs on campus
like I heard them on campus in elementary school. With
breakdance contests taking place at the end of the hallways,
meeting new kids, and noticing that I was becoming increasingly attracted to girls, this was much better than my
earlier elementary school experiences! Racism during this
time of my life was off-campus and I would see more and
more of it in the streets. In those days kids played outside a
lot and many of us would play outside until the streetlights
came on. We had great times amongst the dark shadows
of racism, and until it was blasted in your face, you would
never think that it existed. My curiosity during these years
and a feeling of more independence took me to explore the

greater neighborhood. Rather than just the few couple of blocks surrounding my home that I knew like the back of my hand, I was exploring and navigating all over South San Francisco as far west as the coastal beaches and as far east to the hills of the iconic "South San Francisco, The Industrial City" sign that is stamped into the hillside.

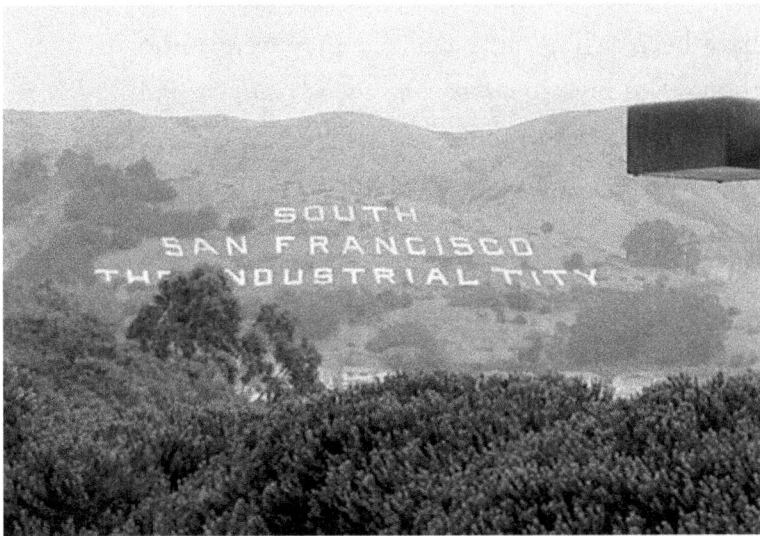

This is when I would begin to see recurring graffiti on light poles, stops signs and often boarded-up businesses. This graffiti was different from the artistic, stylistic and raw graffiti that I would see in downtown San Francisco, Los Angeles, Oakland, or on TV shows featuring New York. It was plain, very unartistic in style and often in thin black, blue, or red letters and it always read, "N-I-G-G-E-R-S

G-O H-O-M-E." When I first saw this crude art, NIG-GERS GO HOME (NGH) scrolled onto varying surfaces from the walls in public restrooms to benches on public bus stops, it meant nothing to me. It didn't really hit me until a car full of white boys passed me by screaming NIGGER! The first time that happened I was by myself, and I looked around to see if there was anyone else around that they may have been yelling at. I realized they were yelling at me! I thought to myself, *damn, they sound really angry! Do I know them?* The tones of their yells sounded as if I killed their pet or something and I couldn't understand the reason for such anger! From that point on, and dozens and dozens of times thereafter, I would experience being called a nigger by white boys driving past me. And every time I saw NGH graffitied somewhere, I began to realize I was the target of this phrase. But what did it mean? What did they mean by NGH? Did it mean that they wanted me to go home to my house where I was growing up? Did it mean they wanted me to go back to the predominantly black Fillmore neighborhood in San Francisco where I first lived? Did it mean to go and live with my father who had since divorced my mother a few years prior? Did it mean going back to my mother's hometown where she was raised in Texas? What did NGH mean? At the time, I couldn't fully comprehend the phrase until I got older and more exposed to black history in America.

Much of the impact of these incidents was the emotion behind how NIGGER was said by white people. When I was called a NIGGER, it sounded as if the people who said it were very, very angry with me or hated my guts (that was a popular phrase that was used when we were kids, "I hate your guts," but it only meant we were mad at our friends or siblings for only a few minutes after a little childhood spat), whereas when derogatory terms were used against other minorities, it sounded like the white kids were joking around laughing and teasing. But being called a NIGGER seemed a bit more personal! If you had ever seen those old news video clips from the 1960s when whites were protesting against the integration of black children and white children going to the same schools, you would have seen white people angrily displaying their hate towards Black Americans. However, most of the time in my experiences you wouldn't see the faces of these racist drive-by linguistic assaults, as these cowards would drive by at high rates of speed where you could only get a quick glimpse.

GONE SWIMMING

If you are familiar with the awkward feeling of going swimming, you are not alone, especially if you are black. I never was a fan of water sports such as swimming, canoeing, boating, etc. My mom put me in swim lessons summer after summer, but I never learned how to swim. I was petrified of water outside of the bathtub. My uncle had a boat and he used to take us to the Bay to fish. Although I went reluctantly, I typically remained in the middle of the boat with my life vest strapped on extremely tight! On one boat outing in the Delta, I finally mustered up enough courage and decided to get into the water with my cousin with my snug tight life vest on. But my uncle took off in the boat, leaving us bobbing up and down in the water. I was asking my cousin, "Is your dad coming back? This shit is creepy". I couldn't see the bottom, let alone my own feet. He did come back. It wasn't until I was about 13 years old that I taught myself how to swim. It was an extremely hot summer day, and we were visiting another uncle and cousin in Arizona.

My cousin, who is a year or two younger than me, knew how to swim and she made it look really easy. From that moment on, and while we were visiting, I had taught myself how to swim. Swimming gave me a sense of anxiety, not only with not knowing how to swim or being a poor swimmer. It was more like, *okay, when we go to this pool, will there be a lot of people? Will it be a lot of white people?* As a kid, I saw in the movies during a pool scene that as soon as a black person entered the water, all the white people would get out, which I would interpret as NGH. That would always be on my mind, and the sad thing about it, till this very day, it still is! Whenever we go to a community pool I have a habit of paying attention to the white people and seeing if any folks get out of the pool when we get in. Notice the photo, this pool was full of people prior to us arriving.

Figure 1 Mid-80s, Summertime, Arizona, all have left the pool!

On one occasion, we made reservations to go camping at a resort and the employee I was making reservations with mentioned there was a swimming pool at their resort. My mind immediately went to wondering if there would be any white folks there who would be offended by us if we decided to go for a swim. Would they get out? In more recent times, my wife and I decided to take a weekend trip to Monterey. We checked into the Monterey Plaza Hotel and settled into our room. We decided we would go up to the spa and soak in the hot tub. The hot tub was fairly large and only one other couple was there. We got into the hot tub on the opposite side of the other couple, who by the way was an older white couple. And then it happened. As soon as we got in, they gave off a strange disgusted look and climbed out of the tub. At first I felt a bit offended, but then I was happy they got out as we now had the hot tub to ourselves. But what really kills me is that these people were probably the ugliest, most out of shape, horrendous looking pair! They made their swimsuits ugly! My wife and I, young and fit, maybe caused them to feel a bit insecure. I know these kinds of folks think you want their ugly ass wives anyways! No thanks! If I was a racist towards ugly, I most definitely would have not gotten in the hot tub in the first place. Perhaps the old couple in Monterey thought they were still in the 1950s, or perhaps things just haven't really changed that much.

"In 1964, several white and black protesters jumped into a pool at the Monson Motor Lodge in St. Augustine, Florida, in what The New York Times described as a "dive-in". A white police officer in plain clothes jumped in to arrest them. The United States has a long history of people of color facing harassment and racism at swimming pools. In 2018, "a black boy was harassed by a white woman in South Carolina as she told him he did not belong at the pool; a black woman was asked to provide identification by a white man in North Carolina; and a black man wearing socks in the water had the police called on him by a white manager of an apartment complex in Tennessee" (Chokshie, 2018).

In New Mexico, during the 1950s, the grandson of a white man who owned a public pool recalled: "The sign on the outside of the pool read: Hours 10am to 6pm Tuesday through Saturday. Colored: Sunday from 1pm - 5pm. After 5pm on Sunday, my grandfather would drain the pool (125,000 gal.), and on Monday, everyone would grab buckets of liquid chlorine and scrub the entire pool. I asked my grandfather why we did this, and he said that the colored people were unclean and this would kill any bacteria that they would bring in. I also would ask my grandmother if I could go swimming on Sunday and she would always tell me no because that was the time when the 'colored folks' could swim, and I wasn't allowed to swim with them" (Costello/ Douez, 2017).

In regards to swimming, about half of the members in my family knew how to swim. However, my mom did not know how to swim as well as many black friends of mine. My father knew how to swim and so I asked him how he had learned. He said that he was thrown into the water by his cousins and like many other Black Americans during his time, being thrown into rivers and bayous was how they learned how to swim. My dad further stated that there were no swimming pools or swimming lessons available to them during the 1940s and 1950s in Crowley, Louisiana, where he grew up. I always wondered why so many Black Americans did not know how to swim.

"Cynthia Billhartz Gregorian reported on a USA Swimming study that found that Black Americans are much less likely to know how to swim than White Americans. Specifically, the study found that only 30 percent of African-American children know how to swim, compared to 60 percent of white children. More alarming, a 2008 study by USA Swimming found that black children are nearly three times more likely to drown than white children. In looking for the causes of this disparity in swimming and drowning rates, it is necessary to look into the past-to the nation's history of racial discrimination.

Swimming as a recreational activity boomed in popularity during the 1920s and 1930s, when cities and towns throughout the United States built thousands of swimming pools. Many of these pools were larger than football fields and surrounded by concrete sun decks, grassy lawns, and artificial sand beaches. By the end of the 1930s, swimming pools had become the most popular form of summertime recreation in many American communities. All Americans, however, did not have access to these pools. Public officials and white swimmers throughout the United States segregated and excluded Black Americans. In large cities, black residents typically were relegated to small 'Jim Crow' pools. In the smaller cities and towns that had only one pool, black residents had no pool in which to swim. The primary cause of racial segregation and exclusion at municipal pools was mixed-gender use. White people did not want black men interacting with white women at such physically and visually intimate public spaces. This racial discrimination severely limited black Americans' access to swimming facilities. In 1940, for example, Black Americans constituted 14 percent of the city's population but accounted for less than 1 percent of swimmers in municipal pools. As a result of limited access to swimming facilities and the austere design of 'Jim Crow' pools, swimming did not become integral to the recreation and sports culture within African American communities. By contrast, swimming became astoundingly popular among whites during the interwar years and developed into a self-perpetuating culture that persists to the present. Each successive generation of white parents takes its children to swimming pools and teaches the children to swim" (Wiltse, 2010).

Now I have an idea of why so many blacks do not know how to swim, America's history of discrimination and segregation at its swimming pools!

THE POST AND BLM

I want to share with the reader a Facebook post that my white childhood neighbor shared in response to the George Floyd murder. Why did I entertain and decide to make a comment to this post? Well, I felt that the poor guy needed a bit of education. However, the reply back ignored my comment and the response he gave was off-topic. Typical! I should have known better. This is what happens when Black Americans try to express the truth, only to be ignored or at least down- played.

Let me take a pause for a minute before I get into that post. Breaking News! I swear I cannot make this stuff up. Another post just hit my Facebook feed, which fits right into what I just mentioned about our experiences being ignored or down-played. A childhood friend of mine, who is a Black American, just posted, "I've lost patience. I am tired of explaining racism to adults. By now, you either already know better and are being obtuse or you need to do the work. And I am beyond tired of being surprised (in a bad way) by the comments/posts of folks I thought I knew. I have accepted that my words will not miraculously change the ignorant. Life is really too short. I'm not mad…just done". I mean, I just got through saying, "Why did I entertain and decide to make a comment to the post?" This is direct proof of what my friend just said. Listen, we are tired of explaining! Especially when we continue to go unheard, doubted or given alternate explanations for our own experiences. As if we are too sensitive and dumb to get what we are going through.

Anyway, back to his original post (fig 2.), which stated: *"People, look at the Black on Black homicide percentages, where is Black Lives Matter on this issue??"* Do we seriously need to explain this to these folks, who are being obtuse like my friend had mentioned who has lost her patience? What is even more absurd is that this way of thinking is even held by various political leaders. It is crazy. I can give a pass on this for the average citizen and their ignorance, but political leaders, no! I don't have much more than a Bachelor's degree and I am sure many of these political folks have much more education than I do. At least I hope they do. From the current looks of things, it seems like they don't have much more than a fifth-grade education and an abundance of wealthy "hammy-down" privilege. Folks like these got a lousy post-graduate education if they cannot recognize and empathize with cultural differences. If you find yourself a bit confused, I strongly suggest you politely ask someone who is articulate and intimately connected with the knowledge and struggles of black life in America, and most importantly, who "gets it". My quick response to this (and to shed a bit of light onto the ignorant) is to start with the killing of Black Americans by cops. I am sure that most folks understand that the police job is a paid civil servant job. It is the citizens of America that pay taxes, which funds police services. In theory, the police work for the CITIZENS of this country. Yes, Black Americans are citizens too, so just like everyone else, Black Americans are entitled to the age-old police slogan "to protect and serve." Black lives matter just like the rest of the citizens of America who look to the police for their protection and service. When you have continuous, unjustified killings of Black Americans by paid civil servants, then you are living in a Nazi America. By the looks of things, America is under the leadership of a new-age Hitler.

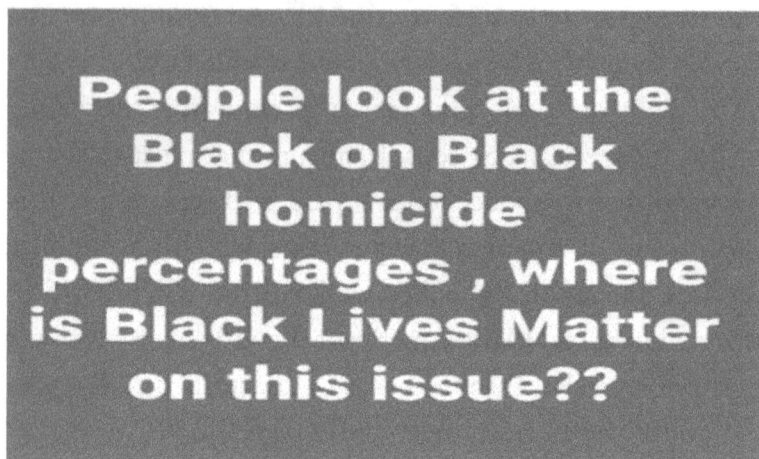

Figure 2 The Social Media Face Book Post June 2020

Politicians like the ex-Mayor of New York said the same. What about black-on-black crime? No wonder this dude is the president's attorney! This statement alone suggests that Black Americans are not concerned with crimes committed by other blacks against them. "Claims like Mr. Giuliani's aren't just offensive or misplaced, they're demonstrably wrong. While Black Lives Matter receives deserved attention, countless grass-roots organizations, many of which were founded by bereaved black women, are doing remarkable work to prevent and reduce crime" (Streeter, 2016). The killings of Black Americans against other Black

Americans, hundreds of senseless killings in black communities perpetrated by blacks, can be considered twice as devastating as Black Americans falling victim to senseless killings by cops, which is profoundly disgusting. The question further suggests, why don't Black Americans make a big deal about this? The answer to this question is Black Americans *have* made issues with black-on- black killings and continue to do so. There have been many marches, movements and protests throughout this country pleading with the American government to help end the violence. Most of the time, these voices go unheard. Black Americans have been abused and killed by White Americans for centuries and when it is suggested that cops be excused or ignored for their acts to kill unarmed innocent Black Americans, we are baffled, especially when statements like this are made by politicians. When whites commit crimes against one another it is never referred to as white-on-white crime, as if whites do not commit any. White people commit crimes just like any other person within any other racial group. From petty crimes to murder, whites commit them. Usually, the crimes that whites commit against another human being are typically against another white person. The killing of another human being is the most immoral act one human can impose on another, and for the families and loved ones of the murdered, we all grieve the loss. I ask and ponder, would it be "normal" to the average White American family to have known or had more than two family members or friends murdered in their lifetimes? In the Black American family, many of us have known more than a few close loved ones who have been murdered.

Personally, I have had close family members and friends murdered by gun violence or some other form of violence. Here are a few of their names: Melvin, late 70s, family friend shot to death; Joya, late 70s, cousin shot to death; James, early 80s, friend from across the street, three of his family members shot to death; Kofi, early 90s, very close friend shot to death; Bobby, late 90s, close friend shot to death; Terrance, 2001, cousin/like an older brother to me poisoned to death and robbed. I ask again, would this be considered normal? A killing is a killing, whether by a cop or a criminal. And because of all the black-on-black killings in the 80s and 90s, it is something that I can say felt inappropriately "normal". But for the hired civil servant, the act of a senseless killing of a Black American will never be considered normal or even inappropriately normal.

I have come to the conclusion that it has been accustomed to American policing and law to such an extent, that it often seems it has been a legal way to kill Black Americans. The post I mentioned earlier posed the question, "where are Black Lives Matter on this one"? Do you folks realize that organizations such as the Newark Anti Violence Coalition and many others have come into existence to address black-on-black homicides? Black communities all across the country have come together to demand justice and help from local to federal governments. "But this local organizing goes largely unnoticed by politicians, scholars and news media, all of which focus on larger national groups with big budgets and expensive lobbyists" (Streeter, 2016).

In Philadelphia alone, there were at least 50 local organizations involved in anti-crime politics in the early 2000s. Mother in Charge, for example, was started in 2003 by Dorothy Johnson-Speight after her son Khaaliq Jabbar Johnson, 24, was killed in an argument over a parking spot. One of the organization's main goals is for Congress to declare homicide a public health crisis. In Newark, Nakisha Allen, 35, was killed in crossfire in July 2009 as she walked to a neighborhood store. Soon after her death, African Americans and Latinos from the city, along with clergy members, activists and local community groups, rallied at the intersection where she was shot, stopping traffic for hours. This was the first demonstration of what became the Newark Anti Violence Coalition, which protested against homicide for almost three years afterward" (Streeter, 2016).

Here are just a few more non-governmental organizations that are in existence behind crimes committed against Black Americans, whether it is black on black, white on black, or a cop killing a Black American:

Mothers of the Movement was created due to the acquittal of George Zimmerman after killing Trayvon Martin in 2013, to spread awareness of police brutality in the US.

Mothers Against Police Brutality (MAPB) is an organization developed in Texas in 2013 by the mother of Clinton Allen, an unarmed young black man who was killed by police. The focus of this group was to change the use of deadly force policy throughout the United States.

Purpose Over Pain, established in 2007 by the mother of a young Black Man murdered in Chicago, which is a group of mothers who go out and post reward fliers.

Mothers/Men Against Senseless Killings (MASK); established in 2015, this group focuses on violence prevention by putting eyes on the streets to interrupt violence and crime by getting out on the streets and by bringing people together through food and spreading love and getting community members to create friendships rather than enemies. Food insecurity, and housing, and to ensure community members have access to necessary services and opportunities for education, professional skills growth, and economic development.

Pico National Network, a faith-based organization in existence since the early 1970s, started the "Live Free" campaign, which is a movement created to address violence and crime. The movement's focus is committed to dismantling the mass- criminalization of people of color.

When people question whether or not Black Americans are concerned about crime committed against each other and assume that they are not, it is a testament to their ignorance and/or lack of empathy or a total absence of it. But my question to the ones that ask such a ridiculous question, why the fuck do you care anyway? Because if you really did, you wouldn't ask the question in the first place. Black Americans are tired and have been tired of senseless killings since slavery. Period. No matter who commits the killing. If people are unwilling, show a lack of care, or are just too lazy to do the research, then America does not need your insensitive and low-intellectual opinions on such matters.

Criminals come from every walk of life, and just like in the black community, there is crime in the white community. This criminal behavior is learned behavior. I will let the reader ponder on this. This learned behavior has its roots in American society, which was not set by Black Americans. The "forefathers" not only set the example and paved the way to an operable and powerful government, but also set the example of how to steal, rape, and murder. I am sure many folks are scratching their heads right now and may be clueless to this truth, and that is why it wasn't taught, only omitted from American history.

In a 2016 article of the USA Today titled, *Why Black Lives Matter doesn't focus on "black-on-black" crime* stated that "Black Lives Matter isn't just about the loss of life, which is always terrible, it's about the lack of consequences when black lives are taken at the hands of police". Again, the police are here to "protect and serve" all citizens as Civil Servants and were not sworn in to murder Black American Citizens!

In response to the post, an Asian female stated, "I grew up in a neighborhood which was of every ethnicity, and we were all friends. I didn't see any racism". Well, I wonder why? I wonder if she realized that not more than 80 years prior, in April of 1942, just one town over in San Bruno, the United States Government opened up the Tanforan Assembly Center. Overseen by the Wartime Civil Control Administration, Tanforan was a temporary internment camp (also known as a concentration camp and more commonly referred to as a detention center) and one of the largest detention centers out of seventeen opened up by the US Government. As Japanese Americans were rounded up and forcibly removed from their homes, they were placed in these detention centers throughout the country. The Tanforan detention center was used to house the San Francisco Bay Area's Japanese American citizens and was used as a temporary site until more permanent camps became available. This detention center was the home of the Tanforan horse racetrack, which featured famous race horses such as the thoroughbred "Seabiscuit". Tanforan held just under eight thousand Japanese Americans during its peak time of operation, which had over one hundred barracks and numerous horse stalls that were used as living quarters by Japanese American families. The living conditions were extremely poor and unhealthy. The "inmates" were subjected to cold, rain and foggy weather conditions, unsanitary horse stalls converted into living spaces. Not to mention numerous insect infestations.

These Japanese American citizens were stripped of their privacy and women and young girls found difficulty with changing and using the restroom. Property such as vehicles were seized and sold and the dignity of these families would be tarnished for life during the next four years. I am sure these four years had a profound and negative impact on generations that followed Japanese American families. The Japanese detention centers in America came to an end on March 20, 1946.

The Tanforan site is currently used as a shopping mall that has been one of the most popular malls in the San Francisco Bay Area since I was a kid. I wonder, does the Asian lady who made the comment on Facebook know what the site of the mall was used for less than 40 years earlier from the 1980s, during the time we grew up in that same neighborhood?

I am sure she must have shopped there on numerous occasions. Maybe she does and maybe she considers racism ended for all Americans with the closing of the concentration camps back in the 40s. This is the type of ignorance held by too many folks here in America who do not understand why organizations such as Black Lives Matter come into existence. The hate of people does not end overnight, and with all the white offspring of those that fought in the war, I am sure they exposed their children to the hate ideology. That's why I often heard the word "gooks" and "chinks" being used by some of the white kids back in elementary school. Later, as an employee for the local Safeway grocery store, the meat department white butcher had very choice words for the Vietnamese cashier whenever he heard his voice over the PA system. The history of the white butcher included being a Vietnam War veteran.

What is undeniably unfortunate, especially coming from Black Americans and non-black minorities, is that some people, while growing up and to this day, perceive and believe that there was and is no racism. I say it is quite peculiar to me that any minority would make such a claim. As if somehow they walk their daily lives as invisible beings oblivious to the greater white community. They walk around blind, deaf, or whatever makes them feel as an equal and unaware and clueless of the covert and overt racism that has plagued communities throughout America. But now that an increasing number of reports of racist attacks against Asians is currently on the rise due to the COVID-19 pandemic, perhaps some are beginning to realize that racism is real and still alive in America for all minorities. If the President of the United States can make racial statements like "The

Kung- Flu Virus," as he rants on blaming and pointing the finger at Asians for being responsible for the COVID-19 pandemic, he is utterly reckless, insensitive, and demoralizing towards Asian Americans. Rather than calling the virus by its given and scientific name, he has the audacity to create and use a derogatory phrase as such, which totally takes me back to elementary school hearing how the little white kids would mock and tease the Asian kids. One must therefore realize that racist statements like these, coming from the most influential and prominent position held in America, has set the tone for the increase in violence against minorities. Citizens have got to undeniably accept the reality that racism is alive and duly noted.

"Amid the ongoing threat of the coronavirus, there are surging reports of xenophobic and racist incidents targeting members of the Asian American and Pacific Islander (AAPI) community in the U.S. Since January 2020, there have been a significant number of reports of AAPI individuals being threatened and harassed on the street. These incidents include being told to "Go back to China," being blamed for "bringing the virus" to the United States, being referred to with racial slurs, spat on, or physically assaulted." (Anti-Defamation League, 2020). In Pasadena, a white motorcyclist attempted to run down an Asian couple who were out for a walk. During the incident, this vicious perpetrator yelled racial slurs while accusing them of bringing the virus to America. In other incidents in San Francisco, a young Asian student was out for a walk and was waiting at the intersection for the crossing lights to change. She noticed a white male across the street yelling at her. As the young lady tried to avoid the confrontation, this vicious and terroristic man decided to get into the young woman's face. As he continued to yell racial epithets at her, blaming her for the virus and encouraging a city bus to run her over, he eventually spat on her. In another incident, a young Asian woman was out walking her dogs when she was told to go back to her country and that "you nasty people need to stay in Asia".

As I am finishing up this section of the book, I happened to tune into the local Sacramento news. It is Monday, July 20, 2020. Over the weekend, a Vietnamese restaurant owner was assaulted by a white customer. The owner of the restaurant had asked the customer to please abide by the rules of the store due to COVID-19, so the customer gets angry with the owner and tells him to go back to China. He yelled some racial slurs at him, and then assaulted him by throwing his drink at him. This is just crazy. These racist folks just cannot help themselves! So, to the sheltered Asian women from our childhood neighborhood, I am sorry to inform you, but racism still exists and has always existed for those who are seen as less desirable and physically different from that of the "founding fathers" of America.

Before the 2020 pandemic, immigrant Mexican and Latin Americans were the focus of the President's racial attacks. As I recall, he referred to them as being criminals, gang-bangers, and rapists. With all the anti-minority hysteria conceived and perpetuated by racist white America, minorities must understand that this traditional racist white American behavior often leads to and results in terrorist attacks. From racial slurs to physical assaults and in some cases to murder, we are all at risk if racist white America continues to blame and accuse minorities of the country's downfalls and its issues. All minority groups of America have had significant negative racist attacks unduly perpetrated against them and/or their ancestors at some point in time in American history and it should be at no surprise to anyone why we are seeing what we are seeing today regarding racial issues. America has never addressed the racism issue head on. Even in Germany where the evil atrocities took place in a campaign to destroy and eliminate all Jewish people, in current times it seems that the citizens of Germany have rectified those racial differences of the past and have moved on from those racists' sentiments, allowing for some sort of healing.

In America, the virus of racism seems to have laid dormant and now the sentiments of racist people have crawled out from the cracks and seems to continue unchecked by the current government. If continued to go unchecked, there will undoubtedly be more division, more hate and unfortunately more loss of life. We hope this does not turn into a modern-day Holocaust in the "Great" United States of America. However, with the ignorance of those who believe that racism does not exist or that people are not concerned with the murder of their fellow citizens and loved ones, we need to be aware and educated on how such evil groups such as the Nazi's rose to power.

THE DENTIST

L ife in Westborough wasn't just about racist white boys. As a matter of fact, one of my best friends whom I am still very close with today is white. I consider him like a brother and his family as my family. Although there were a handful or more of racist white kids, not all whites in that town were racists. However, with all of the other Black American families in Westborough, it gave me the sense that this was HOME and that I did have a sense of belonging. Now that I was able to get around much more and know the greater neighborhood, I was becoming more independent with my comings and goings. I used to walk to junior (middle) high school from time to time, which was about a 30-minute walk from home. Otherwise, my friends and I would take the bus or get a ride from one of our parents. I bring up my 30-minute walk because it brings back lots of fond memories, as well as one that was not so fond. If you are from the Westborough area and were there in the 80s, you will recall the two sinking homes next to one

61

another. These homes literally were sinking into the earth. The back of these houses was tilting and sliding under the earth while the front of these homes began to face more and more towards the sky. One rumor at the time was that a lady from one of these houses was doing dishes when her house started to sink and flew out of the kitchen window! The homes were demolished and only one house is left standing on the short block that used to have three homes.

On the way to or coming home from junior high, if we had a little bit of money, we would make a quick detour to the new McDonalds to get my favorite caramel sundae with (of course) extra caramel! However, I was frequently at the dentist due to cavities. My Dentist (let's call him Dr. G) had his office on the path to my school. In between school and McDonalds was the location of his office. Dr. G was a white man who looked a bit like President Jimmy Carter. His tone was pleasant and he appeared very friendly. As I recall, Dr. G was always smiling.

My memory of Dr. G was not because of his pleasant and friendly appearance, but because of the unpleasant experiences I had sitting in his dental chair getting cavities filled. I had never had any fillings done prior to visiting Dr. G, so he was all I experienced at the time. Extreme pain is what I went through every single time I got a filling. You would think I would stop eating candy and sweets after the first time; however, I didn't learn my lesson. In order to do the filling, the dentist has to prepare you for the procedure, which means he has to numb your gums. My experience with the procedure was extremely painful, and as I write this, I feel the tingling sensations going up my spine and into my brain. Of course, I am in no pain now, but remembering that pain still affects me to this very day! I wasn't then and never have been the type of person to express pain. I always held back the tears during any painful experience in my life. And as much effort as I put into holding back the tears, I remember I always lost at least one during the procedure under the care of Dr. G. I would be truly upset with myself for letting the tear escape, which led me to the feeling of being "weak". It seemed that I was the only kid in that office that was experiencing distress.

Later in life, I would find out that this pain is totally avoidable. In my adult life, low and behold I have a damn cavity. Time for another filling! Oh, hell no! But now, I know I can handle the pain of the procedure. On the way to my appointment, I had a high degree of anxiety and anticipation! As I get into the dental chair, my palms are sweaty and my left leg and foot fidgety. As the dentist begins the procedure, before I know it, he is done! Now I am thinking, *what happened to the pain? Where did the pain go?* I experienced no pain! I am feeling mixed emotions: confused and delighted at the same time. Did dentists get better and more improved? Maybe as a kid I was much more sensitive and now perhaps I could have handled the pain much better as an adult. I felt absolutely nothing! I asked, "how come I didn't feel any pain?" The response I got was, "Because we prepped you with topical, so you shouldn't feel anything". Later, the topic comes up again about the procedure of getting fillings and the pain associated with it. I am talking to my hygienist and I tell her my story with Dr. G. She immediately tells me that he could have lost his dental license for doing that to me! I figured it out! Dr. G never used topicals on me in order to prepare my gums for the shot! Was this dude experimenting on me to see the type of reaction he could get out of me? Was he putting me through unnecessary pain, or worst yet, was he purposely torturing me because he was a racist? Looking back, I would have to say with a bit of certainty that he was! I was just a young innocent black boy at the hands of a white medical professional. I wonder, was this common practice? How many dentists throughout this country would practice torture onto unexpecting Black Americans?

My ex, who is a dental assistant, had started working for a new dentist around 2010. After spending about a week with this new dentist, she realized that he was not applying the topical on black patients. She informed the dentist that she knew what he was doing and how unethical his behavior was, so she ultimately quit working for him. Was this dentist doing the same, practicing torture on unaware black patients? Was Dr. G sending me an indirect message of racism, a hatred towards Black Americans as he injected that huge needle into my gums numerous times without using topical? I have to say with a profound, hell yes! That asshole was purposely torturing me because of my skin tone! As if he was speaking to me telepathically, telling me, NGH!

After a bit of research and looking into medical practices related to Black Americans, I have learned that torturous and experimental medical practices have been quite common and still can be seen today. "The experimental exploitation of African Americans is not an issue of the last decade or even the past few decades. Dangerous, involuntary, and non therapeutic experimentation on African Americans has been practiced widely and documented extensively at least since the eighteenth century...Dr. Sims dedicated his career to the care and cure of women's disorders and opened the nation's first hospital for women in New York City. This innocuous tableau could hardly differ more from the gruesome reality in which each surgical scene was a violent struggle between the slaves and physicians and each woman's body was a bloodied battleground. In other human medical experiments, the recruitment of blacks and the poor is a tacit feature of the study because they recruit subjects from heavily black inner-city areas that tend to surround American teaching hospitals. Even more recently, the segregated nature of U.S. medical training emboldened some physicians to speak with candor of misusing black subjects. '[It was] cheaper to use Niggers than cats because they were everywhere and cheap experimental animals" (Medical Apartheid, The Dark History of Medical Experimentation on Black Americans from Colonial Times to the Present, Harriet A. Washington, First Anchor Books, 2006). This book is a must-read as its revelations of medical practices conducted on Black Americans speak shocking and horrible truths of unimaginable nightmares!

Black American patients have suffered because of the color of their skin at the hands of racist medical professionals who have historically given much less quality care to them than white patients. Black Americans have been used as human "lab rats" at the hands of these doctors experimenting with their lives while sparing the lives of White Americans. As in the case of my experience with Dr. G, I would say it wasn't necessarily the lack of care or any experimentation other than the pure evil of a person willingly and knowingly putting another human being through some sort of torture, pain and suffering. I am sure torture, pain and suffering have been common practice for those bigoted health care providers for hundreds of years as they perform thousands of daily procedures on unaware and unknowing people of color who look to these health care providers for accurate diagnosis, safe and effective treatments and sincere and compassionate follow-up.

"African-American patients tend to receive lower-quality health services, including for cancer, HIV, prenatal care and preventive care, vast research shows. They are also less likely to receive treatment for cardiovascular disease and are more likely to have unnecessary limb amputations. As part of "The 1619 Project," Evelynn Hammonds, a historian of science at Harvard, told Jeneen Interlandi of The New York Times: 'There has never been any period in American history where the health of blacks was equal to that of whites. Disparity is built into the system" (Frakt, 2020).

Back during my college years, I remember learning about the Tuskegee Experiment, where Black American men were injected with syphilis to be studied by American doctors. The goal of these doctors was studying the effects of this disease without providing treatment. "From 1932 to 1972, the Public Health Service tracked about 600 low-income African American men in Tuskegee, Alabama, about 400 of whom had syphilis. The stated purpose was to better understand the natural course of the disease. To do so, the men would be lied to about the study and provided sham treatments. Many needlessly passed the disease on to family members, suffered and died. In 1997, President Clinton and Vice President Al Gore helped Herman Shaw, 94, a Tuskegee Syphilis Study victim, during a news conference. Mr. Clinton apologized to black men whose syphilis went untreated by government doctors." (Frakt, 2020).

My life experiences with some health care practitioners throughout the years have made me somewhat distrusting of the American health care system. The lack of concern regarding my own health with doctors, to my experience with the dentist and the history of the Tuskegee Experiment has contributed to my lack of trust. As folks every year flock to get their flu shots, I remain hesitant and cautious. In all my years, I have gotten the flu shot once back in 1998. That winter, I got the flu pretty bad. Since then, I am torn and conflicted. As a responsible Black American parent, I am even more torn and conflicted about getting my children vaccines.

As we are bombarded with the daily TV ads for medications for this, and medications for that. From physical to mental health, the average American should be overwhelmed with all this TV ad drug pushing! And the majority of these drugs have serious side effects! The one that really annoys me the most is the PREP commercials. Is this an experimental drug targeted at minority individuals? If you all do not know what PREP is used for, it is used to prevent one from contracting the HIV virus. In these ads, gays, transgender folks, and people of color are targeted, especially blacks. What also really annoys me is that rather than promoting other safe sex options such as condoms, these ads seem to promote people to have sex without condoms to using PREP as the alternative preventive measure for contracting HIV. These ads do not highlight monogamy, but rather people out socializing and having a great time! This implies that if you are not monogamous and you are having sex with multiple partners, then don't worry about having to use condoms when you can take PREP. I ask myself, what about all of the other STDs out there that these ads are not addressing? Although these ads follow-up with the side effects such as possible life-threatening issues, these ads are brilliantly put together to show people out and enjoying the time of their lives! The more people who are portrayed as enjoying something, the more that consumers will not heed to the warnings. This will potentially put these target audiences at greater risk and more likelihood of developing this disease and the life-threatening side effects. And if you do not follow the use instructions of these drugs to the "T," you still may end up getting HIV. You can be a perfectly healthy person, but if these ads convince people to throw out the condoms, either way, you are subjecting yourself to becoming unhealthy due to the possibility of getting HIV or developing a life-threatening side effect. No matter what, it would seem to me that if you are in good health, you would be gambling with trading in a perfectly healthy body for one that is not. It makes me question, why? Why are gays, transgender, and people of color targeted? I don't think it takes a rocket scientist to figure this one out!

HIGH SCHOOL

Westborough was located on the west side of South San Francisco and my high school and girlfriend at the time were located on the east side of town (about a 15-minute drive and a 45-minute walk). Before I had a driver's license, I walked a lot or took the bus. Because I was on foot, there were many, many more instances of racial "drive-byes," where I was the victim of "Fuck you Nigger," or just "Nigger". But more notably, there was one group of white boys that worked out of an auto-body shop several blocks north of my high school and about a block south of my girlfriend's home. I typically walk on the opposite side of the street from this business. The first time as I am minding my own business and walking by myself, I hear voices yelling "NIGGER!" I look across the street and there is a group of college-aged white boys staring at me outside of their shop while flailing their arms about. This street was very wide and busy with cars, so I felt I was at a safe distance away from these racist boys. Each time I had to walk that route, if those boys were there (which was at least 70 percent of the time), they would yell "NIGGER" as I passed by.

One day a sense of boldness came over that group of boys. I realized that one of them was a neighbor of my ex-girlfriend, who had never said anything to me while he was alone without his boys. I figured it was because he did not have his group of friends with him. However, as I was leaving my ex-girlfriend's house walking towards the high school, the group of boys spotted me from about a block away and began speeding down the street in a car coming in my direction. The car they are driving makes an abrupt stop right in front of me, and at least five white boys, including the neighbor, jump out, some holding bats. As they are approaching me, they are saying to me things like, "You fucking nigger," "Nigger go home," blah blah blah, as they begin to surround me. Now pause for a minute. I am only in the 10th grade at this time and these dudes are college-aged. I guess it made them feel more confident in approaching me. One finally says, "We are about to kick your nigger ass!" What was I to do? Do I run? Do I yell for help, or do I stay and try to fight off five angry white boys with bats? Then I thought, they say if you run from animals that it incites the animal to chase you, and to me, it would show cowardness on my part. Although I knew I could outrun them, being the fastest sprinter in elementary school, I decided that I would "stand my ground". In hindsight I wonder, that in that moment of fearing for my life, had I been armed with a gun, would I have been justified in a shooting? We all know the answer to that one. Laughable, to say the least! Not only was I not going to run, but I wasn't going to call out for help either.

I decided I would stay and fight these white boys that wanted to harm me just because I was black. As they began to surround me and tell me that they were going to beat my ass, my comment to them was, "You will probably whip my ass cause it's five against one, but one of you will get hurt, and I will be sure to return with my homeboys". At that moment, the weirdest shit happened! These dudes slowly begin to back up, get in their car, and speed off down the street. I am left standing there like, what the fuck? Shit, I thought, my friends and I were going to be having some fun that night beating down some older dudes. But nothing ever transpired, and from that day forth, those same white boys seemed to ignore me every time I passed by their auto body shop. I guess I was a bit crazy during those days because I started walking on the same side of the street that their shop was on. The harassment from this group had stopped after standing my ground. Had I run, it most surely would have been a continuous game of cat and mouse, but in this situation, I was the Doberman Pinscher!

I am now in high school, meeting new friends, playing football, and because of my earlier years in elementary school, I really wasn't too fond of school. I think my motivation for going was more to socialize, play sports, and check out the girls. I did enjoy my French class and auto-shop. My middle and high school teachers were not cruel or mean as my elementary school teachers were, so I did not have any issues with going to class. These teachers, a handful of them, showed concern for black students and their academics, whereas others could care less. However, I began to experience more and more interactions with the police, and not the kind of interaction you'd think you have when gathering for a social PAL event. During the 80s, as black communities began to be plagued by the crack cocaine epidemic, so did the frequency of my police contacts. Although I was somewhat of a rebellious type, I refused to take part in the use or selling of drugs. However, because of several of my associates, police eyes began to focus on me. I'll never forget officer Eastman. He was cocky, arrogant and on a mission to catch me slipping behind the drug game that I wasn't even part of! My only concern at that time, being young and naïve, was that of a frame-up! My father told me a story of some cops trying to frame one of his close friends back in the 70s, but that will be a discussion for later. Later in life, it would all make sense.

Back to cocky Eastman. This dude was actually watching me and confronting me. He assumed I was a high school drug dealer. He would run into me in the parking lot and at varsity football games, always asking interrogating type questions. Of course, I never had any information, but nevertheless the harassment lasted for several months.

One day, a couple of my black friends and I were called into the office. Typically, that means we must have done "something wrong," or I did something wrong, but it surprisingly wasn't. My homeboy and I and one of our sista friends were all called in at the same time. Would you believe the faculty had chosen us to participate in a college course, where we would take one class on a community college campus one day a week for a semester! We all eagerly agreed and I know for the first time in my school life I felt somewhat like I mattered, like the future of our lives mattered to something or someone more than just our families. But of course, I am always thinking there is a twist and reason for anything and everything that seems positive that falls on my lap without my own personal initiation. I asked myself, *why us?* I thought for a second. Maybe it was because we were all black and needed special help, especially at that time because, like I said before, I didn't care for academics and my grades were always marginal. But then I knew that my female friend was an excellent student who always got good grades. I never found out the true reason why we were chosen. I assume it must have been some mandatory clause in the community to expose young black youth to college in hopes of getting more blacks to further their education.

Whatever the reason, it was a great experience for all of us, and from that point on, I knew I would be going to college. In hindsight, the program worked for all of us as we continued schooling after high school graduation.

My friends and I would ride share to the college campus together. On this particular day, my homeboy was driving and we left our high school and needed to stop by his house. Not more than a block away from the high school, we were getting pulled over. This would be one of my first experiences of being pulled over by the police for absolutely no reason. And I must say there were many, many times that I was pulled over thereafter, so many that I cannot even put a number on it. Of course, most times were for no reason at all. My thinking during this initial encounter was, *we must have done something wrong, otherwise, we wouldn't be getting stopped.* As my mind and heartbeat raced as if I was doing a hundred and fifty on the freeway, the police made contact with us. But it wasn't the whole "let me see your license and registration," it was, "Where are you two coming from?" *I am thinking, are you fucking serious? We are not more than a block away from school,* and we are still on the same street as our school. But before we could even get an answer out, we were being told to exit the vehicle. As we did what we were told, we were questioned again, "where are you two coming from?". So, we simply answered, "From school!". One of the policemen stated, "You two fit the description of an earlier

76

burglary". "You fit the description" would not be the first time I heard this phrase from the police! Nothing further transpired from the encounter, and we continued on.

On another occasion after school, it must have been either my sophomore year or junior year, I decided to go meet up with some other friends of mine at the other school in town, El Camino high school. As I approached the school not less than a block away, I was being pulled over. Once again, I am thinking, *what did I do wrong?* I was not speeding, didn't run any lights, no traffic violations that I could imagine or anything that I had done wrong. I am thinking, *do I fit the description again?* Well, no, that wouldn't be the theme of this pull-over! This time it was, "Where are you going?". My response was, "To meet up with some friends". I didn't ask why I was pulled over, so then the officer wanted to see my license and registration. He has my information at this point and tells me to wait a minute as he retreats to his patrol car. Minutes later, he returns and tells me, "You know, you people need to move out of the area and head towards Sacramento". Now I am confused. Why would he be telling me this? But I am also thinking for the first time, is it because I am black? Just a few years ago, I recall that whites were the ones that were moving up north and further east or merely out of state to places like Washington and Oregon. What was the cop trying to tell me? Did it have anything to do with all the trashy graffiti I observed in my early grade school years, NGH? Was this his way of telling me as a young black youth that whites didn't want us here? The feeling I left with after that encounter was that white authorities don't like blacks, so my anxiety level would begin to grow with each and every police pull-over thereafter.

About a month or so later, I find myself being pulled over in the town of either Millbrae or Burlingame. The stop was uneventful other than my heart pounding. "Driver's license and registration," is requested of me. Upon return, after running my information in the squad car, he saw no violations, so no ticket was issued. However, I was told again, "You people need to move out of the Bay Area". Again, did this equate to NGH? I was now convinced Bay Area cops did not like young black men.

However, dealing with unprofessional cops conflicted with my thought that all cops were good people. My parents had a few friends who were black police officers. As a younger kid, I recall one of them coming to my elementary school and speaking to us about the dangers of drugs. In some way, I felt special that I actually knew a police officer. I guess I felt in some way protected and that I actually had a "black-superhero" in our community. Unfortunately, he was tragically killed in a motorcycle accident. I think it was around the same time Marvin Gaye had been murdered by his father. Two black icons that gave me a sense of feeling good to be black were gone just like that! The other family friend was a member of the San Francisco Police Department. An extremely funny man who often stopped by our house to check up on my mom, brothers, and me. He had invited us to some police fair down at Lake Merced just a few miles from home and not far from the San Francisco beaches. There they had different events taking place including canine training shows. It seemed to be the way the police department was connecting with the community. Once we were set to head home, our friend asked if we wanted to ride in his police car and that he would drive us to our car, which was parked quite far away. My mom said okay, and I was excited as I had never been in a police car before. But it wouldn't be the last time! We get into the police car and he says to duct down in the back. As I did, he took off like a NASCAR driver flying down the street, sirens blaring and all. It felt exciting and I felt that the police were all great people. However, as my experiences and encounters with the police began to grow, the less and less I began to look at police as good people. Although the family friends of ours were good people to us, I soon learned that not all black police officers were good as well.

In the mid-1980s I met up with a friend who happened to be over at his girlfriend's house in Daly City. He came from a rough background, wasn't hesitant about getting into fights and had to be a good talker in order to get himself out of precarious situations. Despite all that, he was known as a passionate person, one who enjoyed running cross-country and was serious about becoming successful. As I pull up to his girlfriend's house, my friend is standing out on the front lawn and his girlfriend is at the front door. They were arguing, although I'm not sure what it was about, the argument seemed pretty intense. As we are getting ready to leave the house, the police show up. They made contact with my friend in an aggressive manner and cuffed him. As they are putting him in the back of the police car, he is "mouthing" off to the police. Well, needless to say, he made a collect call to me the next morning from jail. He states the cops had beat him up pretty bad that prior evening. A couple of friends and I tried to visit him in jail, but we were told we could not visit him. My friend had stated that he was bruised up pretty bad and had a swollen black eye. The cops wouldn't allow my friend to have any visits as they were waiting for his injuries to clear up before they would drop the charges and let him go. This wasn't the only person I knew who would be arrested by cops, taken and beaten up.

Not more than a year after this incident, another friend and I were going to record some VHS movies. We had picked up a couple of VCRs, one from my house and another from his. We were on our way to another friend's house when I was pulled over. During the stop, the cop flashed his light into the back seat of my car and noticed the VCRs. From there, he gave me a verbal assault and interrogation about the VCRs. I had told them that the VCRs belonged to us. He continued on with intimidating words of humiliation. I was ultimately given a ticket for window tint and we were sent on our way. I am a teenager minding my own business. What did I do other than being a Black American to warrant such a verbal attack?

THE MOVE

Prior to my first move from the house that I grew up in South San Francisco, one of my first jobs was soliciting newspaper subscriptions as a newspaper salesman. My job was to get people to subscribe to the Bay Area's Times Tribune. I was in no way cut out to be a salesperson, so during that time I made no sales. Although my friend at the time, who had brought me into this job, was a salesperson like no other. Like E40 said, he could sell water to a whale! That's how good this dude was! Every time we went out on a run, he always got multiple sales. Not envious of his sales skills and a total opposite, I hated the thought of trying to convince someone to buy some dumb shit, even though I wanted to make money! The reason I bring up this story is that I couldn't leave this one out...good ole Redwood City!

My first experiences and impressions of this town were before my Moms and my step-father decided to move there in 1988. One of my first assignments on this job, and on this particular day, was to work in the Redwood City neighborhoods trying to obtain subscriptions. I was about 14 years old at the time and eager to do my job. My eagerness was more for the exploration of new towns and neighborhoods, much more than trying to make a sale. Nevertheless, as I made my way around Redwood City, I had never been called NIGGER so much in my life in one day! I'd ring a doorbell, they'd see me and I'd get a lot of "Get out of here, nigger". White men in their driveways, same thing. This day was exhausting! Back then, there were no cell phones or ways of communication. Our boss would give us a xeroxed copy of a highlighted route on a map, drop us off and would return to pick us up 3 to 4 hours later. Sometimes my friend and I worked the same route, but many times we didn't. On the day of my Redwood City experience, I unfortunately worked alone. As I began to realize how much white folks hated me out there, I had nowhere to go and no one to call. It was 3 to 4 hours of pure anxiety as I continued on my walk, often avoiding many houses along the way as I was in fear of some angry white person calling me nigger and perhaps worst, being attacked. The way they expressed hate towards me was like a lion expressing his hate for the hyena. You just never knew what might happen next. Thank God I made it out of there alive. Had it been the 60s or present day, I may have been dead.

After my step-father and mother married, it was decided that we would move from South San Francisco to

Redwood City! Now I am like, *what? Are you serious! Redwood City, oh hell no!* After the experience I had in Redwood City trying to sell newspaper subscriptions, I thought, racist ass Redwood City! I asked Moms, "Why Redwood City?". Her reply was, "I love the weather out there". I was like, "But Moms, that place is racist!". Her response was, "Well, we got to integrate sometime!". In my mind, I'm like WTF! I am not a salesperson, so I am not going to sell my Moms on the idea of not moving to Redwood Shitty (the way I referred to the town after my unfortunate experiences there). If it made Moms happy to move there, so be it! I had to figure out how I was going to survive and deal with a potential onslaught of racial attacks living there.

I thought, I will go buy myself a new Doberman Pinscher, Candy #2. I just knew Candy would protect me if confronted by some racist bullshit. The Doberman Pinscher was my favorite dog due to its tenacious, protective and fearless demeanor. This was my second Doberman Pinscher. Prior to owning these dogs, I learned that they were used in America's Armed Services during wartime. The 1972 film, "The Doberman Gang" left an undeniable impression on my soul, and from there on, I knew I would own one. My first Doberman Pinscher, also named Candy, I had obtained during my middle school years. A family friend of ours bred these dogs and sold Candy to me as a puppy for 150 dollars. I worked a paper route and saved my earnings in order to buy her. A few years prior, our home was burglarized, and not soon after that, my mother and father split. Unfortunately, at the young age of ten or eleven, I witnessed the remnants of our home burglarized: broken windows, turned over dresser drawers and a ransacked home! That night I will never forget, and I recall not being able to sleep at night worrying about someone violating our home while we were in it. When my father split, I felt we had no protector. I was the older brother and now the "man" of the house. But what could a ten-year-old/eleven-year-old do against an intruder?

From that point on, I knew I needed a protector, the Doberman Pinscher. After getting Candy, I trained her to do things that only a young boy would be interested in training them to do. I taught her how to climb ladders, slide down slides at the local parks, and how to climb and jump fences. At the time, I had thought about the German Shepard as a possible protector, but the images of the Watts Riots in the 60s were quite disturbing to me as the police used these dogs to attack Black Americans. I believed that German Shepherds were racist dogs! It didn't help when I would be barked at by these dogs as the police canine units drove past me! It was as if the dogs knew I was black. I knew that my Doberman Pinscher would protect me from the racist German Shepard, or at least that's what I liked to believe. She knew how to fight, I've seen her in many fights and she would tear shit up. The problem was I was too young to know how to get her to stop once she got started.

But back to Candy #2. Before I got her, the move would already be taking place and I would have to convince Moms and my stepfather into allowing me to get another dog.

Not less than a week after moving to Redwood City, the neighborhood youth had a nice welcome surprise for me. Take a guess of what that was? If you guessed a case of beer or welcome to the neighborhood, you are absolutely wrong! But if you guessed a car full of white boys driving by yelling NIGGER as I stood out front, you got it right! Not soon after, they delivered me some food, about a half dozen eggs covering the back of my 1988 Suzuki Samurai Jeep! I am sure they would have been proud to know that the eggs damaged the paint job of my vehicle. I decided I'd spend most of my days back in South San Francisco and San Francisco, while my dog Candy and I navigated through this period of my life. Although I would continue to be pulled over and stopped by the police, I was never pulled over when Candy was with me. Maybe she brought me luck, because I am sure a racist cop wouldn't mind shooting my dog, let alone shooting me. I have had my share of racist encounters all over the Bay Area, but not as intense as Redwood City. Obtaining my dog Candy somehow gave me a sense of comfort knowing she would have protected me if I were ever to be jumped or attacked by some terror seeking white boys.

Later in life, after the birth of my two sons, I encountered yet another racist situation in Redwood City, one which could have had tragic consequences! At the time, my family and I were living with my mom and stepfather at their second, new home in Redwood City. We were waiting for our new home to be built in Sacramento County. One Sunday night after spending a long weekend in Clear Lake, we arrived home around 11:00 pm. Exhausted from the trip, we hurriedly washed up the kids and put them to bed. As I was getting ready to settle in, from the bedroom window that faced the rear of the house, I noticed that the neighbor was having a party. Lots of people were over, and it appeared that they were having a great time in their backyard. Unconcerned, I went to bed and fell asleep fast and hard.

Around two in the morning I am awakened by a loud yelling voice. I can't quite make out what this yelling is all about, but the man seemed to be very angry. I sat up in bed to see if I could hear what he was saying. Because it was summertime and it was warm outside, the window was open. As I am listening and begin to wake up a bit more, I hear this man yelling, "Fucking niggers," "Fuck you, niggers," and many more niggers thereafter. Now I know the dude must be referring to my mother's house, as we were the only black family in the area. I sat there listening to this and I was becoming more and more concerned as his angry sounding voice began to fill with rage. Not understanding or knowing why he was so angry; I am getting even more concerned. After about ten minutes of this, the man goes into his house, and I hear his screen door slam! I am thinking, *okay, this dude must be tired from all that yelling and rage.* Next thing I know, he comes back out of the house screen door slamming again and he starts all over with nigger this and nigger that. From that moment, he states, "I am going to shoot right into you niggers' house," and I hear the unmistakable sound of the racking of a chamber of a shotgun. With my pistol close by, I grab it and wake up my family, sending them all to the front of the house. I tell them to call 911 from downstairs. Making sure all lights are off on the backside of the house, I am peering through the window standing guard. I am thinking, *if this dude follows through with this threat, I am unloading this magazine.*

As I sit covering the rear of my mother's house, it seems like forever before the cops arrive. Once there, I met them in the front yard and explained to them the situation. They proceeded to surround the man's house. Some go through the backyard and over the fence, some speed off in their cars to go around the block to get to the front. They make contact with the man and end up taking him to jail. The crazy thing is, they are telling me that they cannot search his house for the weapon. They book the man into jail for making terrorist threats. They took my statement and questioned me about the chambering of the shotgun and if I was sure I knew what the chambering of a shotgun sounded like. Well, of course I know what a damn shotgun sounds like. I was trained to use one! I knew the guy would probably be bailed out by morning, so my anxiety stayed heightened, and I remained alert. We learned that the man was a racist from other neighbors and that we should be careful with him. Later, I am contacted by the District Attorney's Office, and once again I am questioned about how sure I was about the sound of a chambering shotgun. And just like I told the cops, I told them I was trained to use them. It almost sounded as if they were disappointed that I knew about guns and the fact that I was 100 percent confident. The outcome was that this white man only served a night in jail and ended up getting probation. What a slap in the face after the terror my family and I endured that night!

CRUISING

San Jose, California. To be a black teenager in San Jose during those days, let's just say, be careful! Although I wasn't harmed physically, the potential for it was thick in the air. Out of the handful of times that my friends and I went to San Jose to either join cruising strips and check out girls or go clubbing, harassment was like I had never seen before by cops. There were two places where cruising was popular at the time, and that was Broadway in San Francisco and Santa Clara, or maybe it was Market Street in San Jose. In San Francisco, I was never pulled over during a cruise. The only time I was stopped by the police at a cruise in San Francisco was when a police car ran into me during a high-speed chase. But every single time I went to San Jose, I was pulled over. And those cops at that time in the 80s, working the downtown beats, were rude as fuck. Arrogant and cocky as hell! I always found it quite interesting that hot rods mostly owned by white folks were allowed to cruise anywhere at any time unabated and with a small presence of happy looking cops. I did notice something peculiar, as those happy looking cops passively observed "hot rods", that during minority cruises cops aggressively observed Hispanics and Blacks.

If you are a car enthusiast such as me, you pay close attention to the details of customized hot rods, lowriders and everything else in between. A couple of things really stood out to me as I observed cops and their interactions with hot rod enthusiasts, mostly middle-aged to older white males, and those of low rider and custom car enthusiasts, mostly young Hispanic and Black men. I learned a lot as a youth who customized my own 1988 Suzuki Jeep, adding deep dish rims and tires, which proved to be a California Vehicle Code violation. The violation was that if the fenders of your car do not completely cover the tires of your car, or if they protrude from the frame without adequate fenders, the action is considered illegal. After understanding why it was illegal, it made perfect sense. The reason for the vehicle code was to prevent debris such as pebbles and rocks from being hurdled into traffic on other oncoming cars. Makes sense, right? But I wondered why the same rule did not apply to hot rod roadsters owned by white men. These cars were often customized for the tires to be on the outside body of the frame, meaning there were absolutely no wheel coverings over the tires. Although I did modify my issues with my rims and tires, which were signed off as a fix-it ticket by the police, I still would get harassed from time to time. I have been to several hot rod car shows and cruises, and in the presence of the police, I have never seen a hot rod roadster get pulled over and cited for vehicle code violations. Noticing the minor violations of customized cars of whites and minorities, you quickly see that such minor violations get totally ignored by cops when the cars are owned by whites. The minor violations are aggressively enforced when the cars are owned by minorities.

Loudness was another thing. Whether it was white guys cruising on Harley Davidson bikes with gut wrenching loud exhaust pipes or white guys in hot rods with blaring engines setting off car alarms, it never seemed an issue to happy on looking police. But if you had loud bumping music with deep bass, you were destined to get a ticket at every chance a cop was looking to harass or write you up on a noise violation. I guess certain laws only apply to certain people of color, whereas others are given a pass.

As hundreds of cruisers and spectators showed up in San Jose enjoying fancy cars and the warm summer nights, keep in mind that there was a criminal element amongst the majority of the law- abiding cruisers, but this was a very small group of folks looking to ruin the night of others. I guess Hispanics and Blacks were all collectively seen as criminals, justifying the actions of the police. Needless to say, when Hispanics and Blacks cruised, cops were in full force, pulling anyone over for minor traffic violations to no violation at all. This one particular night that I will never forget. I got pulled over at least five times and threatened at least twice with jail time and a car impound if I did not leave. Would you believe this threat actually came from a black cop, who seemed to have a very bad attitude and hatred towards me proven by his aggressive and intimidating demeanor? This dude was nothing like our family-friend cops back when I was a kid. Like Ice Cube said, "black cop showing out to the white cop," so I understood where that was coming from. Out of those five times I was pulled over, three of those times happened within the same block with different cops each time and each time with harassing comments and questions. Although the allure of pretty girls in San Jose is what originally brought my friends and I to San Jose, I eventually stopped going. I guess the harassment was too much to deal with. To me, this was another NGH experience. San Francisco remained THE spot to cruise until we discovered Sacramento's Broadway, Miller and William Land Parks!

FINDING A JOB

In the early 1990s I decided I wanted to spread my wings and leave the nest, so a couple of friends and I decided to move to Sacramento as roommates. There were five of us from the Bay who were ready to find ourselves by seeking independence. Three of us went to Sacramento and two went to Long Beach. Long Beach sounded like the better choice, but at the time, I had a more solid and supportive plan in Sacramento. Sacramento was a life changer for me. Although I was a "Bay Boy", nothing ever stopped in the Bay. There was always something to do! Sacramento proved boring to me really quick. Lights were out early, and many stores were closed on Sundays. It took quite some time to adjust to the new life in Sacramento. My goals at the time were focused on continuing my education with community college and later transferring to Sacramento State. Although I had no idea on what I wanted to become or what to major in, I stayed in school and pushed myself for two reasons. The first reason was the push of my mother. She was always in my ear about staying in school. She was absolutely relentless in this regard and would never let up. My second reason was due to the racism I was experiencing trying to get a simple job. Damn! As a black man, trying to find a job in Sacramento in the 90s was like trying to win big by playing Super Lotto. My first ridiculous attempt at finding employment was being naïve and falling for one of those sales pyramid type organizations with the promise that hard work could lead to management positions. What a waste of time!

I had worked many jobs in the Bay and it was never hard to find employment there. Prior to moving to Sacramento, I worked for Safeway. I loved my job and enjoyed most of my co-workers. It was a diverse environment and most of us all got along. But despite all the good of the job, racism still found a way to rear its ugly head. Management consisted of the assistant manager (let's call him Joe) and the manager (let's call her Bonnie). Joe appeared to be white, but there was something about his look that seemed ethnic. He was not the friendliest type of guy, and I could tell he did not like me much. Although nothing overtly racist came out of Joe, I could assume there were tendencies by the way he interacted with minority employees. Now Bonnie, a white woman, was condescending, rude and belittling towards us blacks. She definitely came across as a racist. Before I assumed she was a racist, I wanted to give her the benefit of the doubt. However, I did observe how nice she was to the other non-black employees.

I had been working at Safeway approximately two years before Bonnie became our new manager. I was a bagger at the time, more professionally termed as a courtesy clerk. I had put in my time as the lead courtesy clerk. The two other courtesy clerks followed by me regarding seniority were black and the next person down was a white girl (let's call her Becky). Us black courtesy clerks had no issues regarding getting our jobs done and getting to work on time. We were very friendly, courteous and were often offered tips due to our good service. Becky was a really nice girl, but there was a "minor" issue with her. She was an alcoholic! She came to work drunk, and she stayed drunk most of the time while on the job. During her lunch hour, we would often see her at the next-door Straw-Hat Pizza parlor ordering a pitcher of beer for herself. She would finish the pitcher of beer and would stumble right back into work. This went on and on. Management knew about this, and Bonnie was very aware of the situation. However, nothing was ever done. As you could imagine, drunks are often lazy, unsteady on their feet and they slur their words. This was the behavior of Becky on the job. She was drunk so much that it soon became a normal thing, and no one would say anything.

Before Bonnie came to our store, I was going to ask the manager at the time if I could be promoted to a cashier position or to a position in the meat or produce department, but I missed the chance. Once Bonnie came, I decided I would work at least one more year to show her the type of dedicated employee I was in order to increase my chances of obtaining a promotion. So, about a year later I approached Bonnie and politely asked if it was possible to get a promotion. The response I got was, "You come to work, and you do your job. However, you do not go above and beyond your routine duties, so no". I am thinking, *seriously?* I had many choice words for this situation. I was able to gain some satisfaction from the situation although I was never promoted. I had a plan to remedy the issue. My mother during that time had opened a group home for abused and neglected Bay Area children, where she hired me as a group home youth counselor. I remained in touch with my friends at Safeway, and until this very day, some of us remain good friends. After I left Safeway, the two remaining black courtesy clerks would move up to first and second seniority. One had asked for a promotion sometime after I left and was denied like I had been. But low and behold, Becky was promoted to the meat department. Bonnie was so cold that she bypassed the two hard-working black courtesy clerks for the drunken white courtesy clerk. Is it safe to say Bonnie was a racist and that she could be considered part of systemic racism? Well, to many of us, indeed she was. Later, one of the guys transferred to another Safeway store, and the other quit.

Another racist occurrence that took place at Safeway while I was working there happened with a close co-worker and me. The incident took place on one of the grocery aisles. I recall being in the soda and popcorn aisle. How ironic! As my co-worker and I headed to the back of the store to clock out for lunch, we came across another co-worker's mother who was in the store shopping. His mother was carrying her three to four-year-old granddaughter, who I believe was the niece of the other co-worker. My friend knew this lady, so we stopped to say hi and have some small talk. As they began to talk, the little girl with such an innocent face looked at my friend and pointed at him and said to her grandmother, "Look, grandma, it's a NIGGER". My friend and I looked at each other in disbelief. What the fuck! The grandmother, obviously horrendously embarrassed by the red expression on her face, began to apologize at the same time my co-worker was explaining to the little girl that what she had said wasn't nice. Seems racism starts very early in life and without choice. The location of this Safeway where we worked was minutes away from where I lived, the same neighborhood the Asian girl earlier in the book said she had never seen any racism.

Fast forward to Sacramento, and like I said, my sales skills sucked. My first gig was trying to sell water filters and knock-off colognes. I didn't believe in coercing folks into buying bullshit, so needless to say, that didn't work out. I never did make one sale. As fast as I took those two jobs was as fast as I quit those two jobs. I'd say not more than a week. Prior to all the online technology, I am back searching for jobs in the Penny Saver, a small paper periodical that came out each week in Sacramento. One day I came across an ad that mentioned they were hiring at a brand new Food Maxx grocery store in Citrus Heights. This store was huge, three times the size of the Safeway store I worked at, and to me, that meant they would need to fill lots of positions. Now my thinking is positive. My thinking is, *this job is right up my alley, I have experience, three years in the business.* I felt very confident. So, I eagerly applied and waited one week. No callback. Then two weeks. No callback. The store had been within weeks of its grand opening, and I knew they would have to be at least training new employees by now. By the end of the second week, I decided to go to the store. It was almost completed and there were folks that were already working. I sought out the manager to ask about the status of my application. This man told me that I was not selected as I was not a "good fit". I am thinking, *I graduated high school, I attend college, I worked for Safeway, I have no criminal record. What can this rejection be about?* I wondered, was this discrimination at its finest? When I checked that box on the application that asks for your nationality or race, was this the deciding factor that made me "unfit?" As I looked around at all of the new employees that day, I realized something was missing. I did not see any minorities other than one Asian guy. Guess he was right, I wasn't a good fit. So that whole NGH was once again confirmed.

I needed a job to sustain myself! I kept applying to different local grocery stores with no luck, so I kept my job back in the Bay Area as a group home youth counselor until I could find steady work. And people wonder why so many black male Americans turn to crime! But now, I'm hell-bent on not going that route! Eventually I found a part-time job at the mall working in a small department store stocking and steam pressing clothes and preparing them for the sales floor. This paid minimum wage and I only worked about 20 hours per week. I was good with that as I needed gas money!

BLATANT RACISM IN SACRAMENTO

During this time, I was living with two other room-mates and my dog Candy number two in Sacramento. I raised her indoors, so she was always with me until I moved to Sacramento. Because the home we moved in was very small and I had roommates, Candy had to stay outside. I guess Candy did not like it outside as she would bark a lot. This one particular day, I went out to my backyard to bring her in for a bit. As I was out in the yard, a woman from the yard behind me yelled out to me. She said, "Shut your fucking dog up, you fucking NIGGER!". I didn't even know this woman and never had any issues with her. It was the first time I even knew she existed! Well, once she called me a nigger, I had a few loud choice words for her right back, including an onslaught of words that included plenty of "fucking bitches". My Filipino neighbor had heard the whole thing. He later told me, "Hey, I would have cussed her out too!". By this time in my life, I am really sick and tired of folks calling me a nigger!

As I settled into life as a Sacramento resident, I had various run-ins with the "finest" (the police). One day, I was being followed. You know how it is (Black American Men) when the police spot a young black face behind the wheel going the opposite direction and they make that quick U-turn. Of course, you know you've done nothing wrong, so hey, let's get that heart rate up again, let's increase the anxiety level. You know how it is. Intimidation, and for what? Maybe because I hadn't gone "home" yet? Damn, I wonder how many Black American men got PTSD because of this bs! By now I am used to the routine and the routine questions of interrogation. On this particular pull-over I was asked something I had never been asked before, and that was, "You got any bodies in the trunk?". Was this dude joking? Honestly, I did know if he was joking or not by the stern look and the typical arrogant cop demeanor. He eventually let me be on my way.

Some years later, here comes Rancho Cordova PD. Cops seem to have a thing for pulling over blacks in Cadillacs. My late uncle and auntie had this 95 Coupe Deville. I am not really a Cadillac fan, nor would I ever buy one due to the delicate aluminum heads, but this one was clean! One day, my mom and I met up with my uncle and aunt for an afternoon lunch. They picked us up in the Cadillac, which I have always seemed to admire whenever they came to Mom's house to visit. As we are on our way to lunch, I say to them,

"Man, this sure is a really clean car". When my uncle passed away my auntie offered the car to me. So, I have this 95 Cadillac and within a year's span I am pulled over at least four times. Would you believe what I was pulled over for? Absolutely nothing! The typical questions were asked, but one of those traffic stops had me a bit concerned for my life. I was on my way to work, headed for downtown Sacramento. By now I am in my career job. As usual, I am dressed in my suit and tie. It is around 6:30 in the morning. As I head for the freeway, I realize I am being pulled over. Again, I am thinking, *what for this time?* But I already know the routine. As this police officer is walking to my driver's side window, I am watching his hands. I see him reach for his holster, and I am like, damn, *is this fool about to pull his gun?* He unsnaps his holster retention strap and now has his hand on the butt of his gun. I roll down my window and he asks me where I am coming from and where I am going. It's 6:30 in the damn morning and I am in a suit and tie. Even my two-year-old nephew could have told this idiot where I was going. "I am going to work. I just left my house," I replied. The officer said, "Well, you fit the description of a robbery suspect". What the fuck! First of all, some folks will commit a robbery in a suit and tie and dress shoes, but that shit is not common. You may see that on TV, but usually it's white folks robbing folks in suits and ties. How many black men have you seen robbing folks in a suit and tie? Not common!

And if this policeman thought I was a robbery suspect, how come you did not pull me out of the car as a felony stop? You know, "hands out the window, slowly get out of the car, put your hands up and walk backward to the sound of my voice". I thought, that's how you handle an armed robbery suspect. Yep, full of shit! Anyways, he sent me on my way.

Years before that, my brother-in-law at the time and a close friend and I decided we would go to an indoor shooting range in Rancho Cordova to practice some target shooting. My friend had just purchased a brand new 380 and I purchased my first nine-millimeter from some pawn shop on Stockton Boulevard. I was told the gun was made during the time of the Korean War. We head to the shooting range excited to try out our new guns the "legal" way. We had our ammo, purchased some targets and into the shooting stalls we went. This was a first-time experience for us and without ever having any formal firearms training, we burned through our ammo in what seemed like only minutes. The staff at the gun range seemed friendly and a bit informative, which was definitely appreciated, being that it was our first time. All out of ammo, we made our way out of the gun range area, browsed the gun room and headed out to the parking lot to head home.

The gun shop was located in an area of town that was mostly industrial, surrounded by outlying neighborhoods in which we lived. During that time the neighborhood had its share of violence. Murders and criminal activity were the reasons why we decided to buy guns. We headed out to the parking lot towards my friend's late-model gold Regal. It was dark outside and only several lights illuminated the area. As we made our way towards the car, I noticed the sound of a helicopter above, which was quite normal to hear in the neighborhood. We didn't think much of it. As we put our guns away and drove out of the parking lot, I noticed a really bright spotlight pointed not far in front of the car as we approached the stop sign. The next thing we realize, about a half dozen police cars are surrounding us from all angles and I quickly learn that this "ghetto bird" helicopter has its spotlight on us! We stopped in the middle of the street and our car lit up like a Broadway performer on stage! Then over a bullhorn, an officer is giving us instructions. First, they tell my friend, the driver, to get out of the car slowly, walk backwards and lie down on the ground. They cuff him and stick him in a patrol car. I am sitting "shotgun" getting the same instructions. As I get out, hands up, I take a brief glance over my shoulder and see cops everywhere and guns pointed at me. All I can think is, *don't shoot*. Did I say it out loud or in my head? Hell, I don't know. They have me back up, lie down and then a cop engages me, cuffs me, searches me and places me in a separate patrol car. The same thing occurs with my brother- in-law and he was put into a separate car.

Now this was a felony stop, the kind of stop that occurs when a cop believes he has a robbery suspect!

Not once did they say why they were detaining us. Some of the officers proceeded to my friend's vehicle and searched it thoroughly. I noticed that they pulled out all of our guns and set them on the vehicle. We sat in the back of these police cars for about 20 to 30 minutes before there was any communication between the cops and us. As I sat in the back of the patrol car sideways and my hands were cuffed behind my back, I heard several officers talking. They were saying things like, "We can't find anything!" "Nothing," "I am sure they have something," "No drugs," "Not a part of any gangs". All this jibber-jabber. I could tell these cops were frustrated that they didn't have anything on us. We were clean and I could tell that they did not like that. Eventually, they let us go, but prior to letting us go one of the cops told me that the gun range employee had called the cops stating that we were gang members and that, "You guys are lucky you burned through all your ammo. Had you had any remaining in your gun, it would have been a felony". Well, thanks for the education and heads up! Young and dumb, I didn't even realize how much these cops violated us and our rights as law-abiding citizens. And the gun employees must have had bad intentions for us, acting as if they were so helpful with us. They had that smile on their face, but actually had bad intentions for us! I take that as another NGH moment, and as I continue to live and learn and how to navigate through racist American society being black, I become more and more untrusting of American society as a whole.

THE DEALERSHIP

The year is 2002, and as I mentioned, I am now in a solid
career. I have bought my first home and I am in the financial position to purchase a brand-new car. A co-worker
of mine had been telling me that Lexus is the way to go due
to its reliability, power and comfort. I was interested in the
Acura as well, so I set out to go test drive these cars. During
this time, I was living in the Sacramento region but commuting to San Jose to my job every day. I decided to go to an
Acura dealership first. At this particular dealership in Redwood City, I was ready to test drive a new car. Reluctantly,
a salesperson let me take the car out for a ride. The focus of
the conversation was geared around whether I could afford
the car or not. Long story short, the salesman was not taking
me seriously. I liked the Acura and its power, but it wasn't
comfortable, and I needed a comfortable riding car in order
to do the long commute. I continued my car search and decided to visit a Lexus dealership in Sacramento County. As
I entered the clean and pristine lobby of the dealership, I

approached the podium and informed the lady that I was interested in test driving one of their cars. As I looked around, I noticed that I was the only customer in the lobby other than folks sitting in the waiting area waiting for their cars to be serviced. The lady called out on the PA system. "We have a customer in the lobby". A few minutes pass and no one comes to greet me. A few more minutes pass and I notice a rather large white male with white hair and a cop style mustache dressed in a suit coming towards my direction. He had a name tag on with the Lexus logo. Not knowing what his course of business was at the moment, I assumed he was coming over to greet me. Well, he passed by me and walked out of sight, came back and passed by me again as if he looked lost and was getting ready to pass me by for the third time when the lady from behind the podium politely told him that I was the waiting customer. With somewhat of a confused expression, the salesperson reluctantly greeted me as did the salesperson back at Acura. As he came over to me, he did not appear pleased, but more agitated. He asked me what it was I was looking for. I told him the model that I was interested in, and I told him I would like to test drive it. With a bit of annoyance in his voice, he stated he would be right back to take me on a test drive. As we proceeded to the car, there was very little dialogue between the salesperson and me. When we did converse, it was less about the car and more about whether I could afford it. I get that, but I am the type of person that hates shopping, especially for cars! I am not trying to waste his time, and especially not mine.

The whole experience with this guy was horrible to say the least. I did like the car, especially for the comfortability and sound system. I made my decision to purchase a brand-new Lexus, but it sure as hell wasn't going to be from this dealership by the way the salesperson treated me! I decided I would go to a Lexus dealership in the Bay Area. I thought of Serramonte, San Leandro, and Concord. I briefly thought about Redwood City, but I just knew it would probably be just as bad as Sacramento. Weeks later, as I am visiting Moms in Redwood City, I say to myself, *what the hell, let me give Redwood City a chance!* If I feel disrespected or racist tones flare up, I'm out of there! So, I went into the lobby and this salesperson, nicely dressed and much smaller than the guy in Sacramento, approached me. In a very polite and respectful manner, he welcomed me into their store and wanted to know how he could help me. Wow, what a relief! I am treated with dignity and respect, and I am black, all at the same time. Unbelievable! The Asian salesperson had a very easy sale with me. I already knew what I wanted, so I did not even need to look at it or take a test drive. I told him the model and the color, and he got my business. Was I getting a good deal? Hell, I didn't know. At that point, I honestly didn't even care! All I cared about was getting the respect that I felt I was entitled to as a customer, just like any other non-black customer. A special thank you to my Asian brother out at Putnam Lexus of Redwood City back in 2002 for a respectful experience. I truly appreciated that!

However, to that Chrysler auto dealership out in the Bay Area, the respect of your service members towards my father was disgusting! My elderly father loved his Cherokee Jeep.

I would honestly say that this car was truly a "lemon", a piece of shit. It looked nice, but it was horrible! I asked him, "Dad, why did you get that type of car?". Word of advice, people, do your research! This vehicle was brand-new, and it had all sorts of electrical issues. My father could be driving down the freeway when the car would just suddenly shut off, with all electrical power lost! I mean, this could be very dangerous. My dad wouldn't drive this car at night because of this issue. My dad went around and around, trying to get things fixed. The car was so damn new they should have just given him a new one. He could have been killed behind this faulty vehicle! He had been complaining about the same issues for months to this dealer, and every time they would tell him that they could find nothing wrong with the car. One day, I happen to be over at my pop's house and he asks if I would go with him to the dealer in order to drop his vehicle off for the fifth or more times over the same electrical issues. As we enter the service department, I immediately get a sense of what the problem is. It is an unspoken language that clues me in.

By this point in my life, through my own experiences, I know exactly what the issue is. The welcome crew was not so welcoming. It was as if we were not customers, but an extinct people who existed years ago, permanently affixed to the lobby floor as monuments without much notice and full of dust! These people would look right through you! Several employees were acting distracted or too occupied. So, you wait several minutes before engaging. Once they engaged my dad, they asked him what he was there for. He told them he had an appointment for this vehicle. After looking up information on his computer screen, the service guy proceeds to ask my dad what is wrong with the car. Now, after several times you would think these idiots had some clue. What the fuck was he looking at on his computer screen? I am sure they knew why he was there, as there was a history! So, my dad, with frustration written all over his face but with a calm and polite demeanor, explains what the issue is. As my dad is explaining this to him, the guy is looking at my father and asking stupid questions, as if he is looking for clarification or that he couldn't understand my dad. It's as if he was speaking another language. Now I know things are complex, but they had his car numerous times, and they should be telling my dad what they think is wrong by now! This was either extreme incompetence by the service department or yet another overtly racist experience. And that is how they were doing my dad. I quickly got annoyed and loudly expressed my distaste for the car and how I would never do business at this Chrysler dealership. For all the readers that have experienced this, just know, you are not crazy. This is just an indirect form of racism! These people do not want to be bothered with us and you can tell this by their attitudes, behaviors and expressions, which say a lot! When they don't want to talk to you, it is written all over their faces, like they drank some spoiled milk or something. This racist moment is yet another NGH moment. When you experience this, if you can, take your business elsewhere. Do not support racism and do not bother to speak to a manager. They already know how their employees are. Keep a calm demeanor and just leave. If it is one thing racist people like to do is to push us to the brink where we lose our cool and we end up going off or cussing someone out! Remember, they want you to act that way so they can justify calling you an animal or, worse yet, a Nigger. Just leave and be sure to give the business a very bad rating!

My first-born son, an ex-employee of CarMax, had a story to tell me. Prior to being accepted to UC Davis as an undergrad student, he had been acknowledged as a top sales employee. From my son's perspective, in this company, he had confirmed and shed a bit of light on racist attitudes of car dealership employees towards Black Americans. My son explained to me that many of the white employees avoided black customers as they believed black customers either didn't have the money, credit or were not serious in buying. He stated that when some of the white employees saw Black Americans coming in, they would often leave the welcome podium in order to avoid servicing them. My son stated he would most likely be the one to provide the service or another black employee. While servicing a Black American customer in casual dress, because the white employee at the podium left, my son was able to earn a very rewarding commission. This casually dressed Black American bought a luxury car in cash!

It is June 21, 2020, Father's Day. I am in the middle of this book, wrapping up the Dealership and I get a phone call from my brother who does not even know that I am writing a book, let alone talking about the experiences at car dealerships. Days earlier I let him borrow one of my cars as he needed to bring his car in for a service appointment. As we typically talk about his new job working for the United States Post Office, this time, it wasn't about the racism he encounters daily while delivering mail to predominantly white neighborhoods in the foothills just east of Sacramento. This time, it is about his experience at a Ford dealership. As I listen to him describe his experience, I hear in his voice that he's tired, a bit confused and frustrated. He proceeds to explain, "Why, when I go to this dealership, these white men look at me the way they do, with distaste, unliked, and reluctant to greet me?". He further states, "I just want to be treated equally and with respect". He questions, "Why do they treat the white customers with such profound respect?". I kind of give off a chuckle in response, not because it's funny but more because it is typical. This is what we deal with many more times than not when going to car dealerships operated and run by racist people.

The Tip

From time to time, I enjoy dining out. A few years ago, I came across an interesting topic about Black Americans and how they tip restaurant servers. I heard this conversation on a right-wing radio station commentary talk show. I listen to right-wing shit from time to time just to give myself a sense of how "they" are thinking about us and the attitudes they hold regarding Black Americans. Lots of typical stereotyping to say the least! But I had not heard this one prior to hearing it on this particular talk show, about how Black Americans do not tip well. I remember there was a time when tips were just tips. Basically, tips were not required, and as a food server, you had to earn a tip through good, if not excellent service. Tip percentages were never included on your bill receipt. But as we all now know, tips are now commonly required and based on a percentage of your entire meal price. Let me clue some of you guys in who haven't figured this out yet.

This entire book has been about my life and racist experiences occurring under various situations and different scenarios. For the ones that fit the description of those right-wing supporters who say Black Americans do not tip well, did you guys think that racism stopped at the entrances of restaurants? I cannot tell you how many times I have had a server come off rude, condescending and sometimes downright disrespectful and mean! I know many servers, by the display of their attitudes, would prefer not to serve Black Americans because of their racist views. Unfortunately, we get hungry and like to eat just like the rest of Americans. Honestly, I do not get why racist people take jobs where they have to work with and serve others, where they should know they will run into someone that does not wear the same skin color and does not look like themselves. I know folks who have moved to far northern locations like Oregon, Washington and Idaho in order to escape color. But as minority populations continue to grow here in the United States, eventually there will be no place left to escape, as there is no longer a black and white America, in case you haven't been paying attention. "Nine out of 10 rural places experienced increases in diversity between 1990 and 2010, and these changes occurred in every region of the country" (Douez & Costello, 2017). Racist folks are so consumed with hating Black Americans that they don't seem to realize how diverse

America has become, with many folks from many different non-white ethnicities.

Black Americans are often served by racist stereotype-thinking servers, and they cannot help expressing it in many nonverbal and sometimes verbal ways. I will tell you this: dignity, courtesy and respect go a long way when it comes to tipping. If you treat me with anything less than you treated the white customer in the booth next to mine, believe me, you may not get a tip at all. I am pretty sure many people tip this way. Bad and rude service equals no tip! That mandatory percentage means nothing to me if you treat me less than human. I tip according to how you treat me as a customer. I am always polite and courteous the way my parents, uncles and aunts taught me to be. So, for those folks that believe we are bad tippers, think a little bit deeper than that. I promise you it won't hurt!

It was Mother's Day. My mom never really comes to visit us in Sacramento, but this year she decided to come, and I wanted to take her and her grandchildren to this really nice restaurant for breakfast. At least I thought it was a really nice restaurant! Let's call this restaurant "B&B", although the real name of this restaurant suggests an unhealthy menu. As a treat or special occasion, the food is delicious! But customers beware, especially if you are black. There are two of these restaurants in the greater Sacramento area (not to confuse this one with the one-off Broadway, but the other one is close to downtown off J Street). Talk about rude! I was excited that my mom was there and had traveled all this way. I wanted to treat her to something special! If you have a big party at this restaurant, you must order a main course. So, we make the order and add an additional item. The additional item never came so I asked the server if we were going to get it. She was an Asian girl who was acting a bit confused, so I tried explaining the situation to her. I could not figure out why this seemed so complicated and there seemed to be no language barriers. You could see the cooks from where we were seated, and our waitress went to explain to the cook our situation. I am watching the whole interaction between our server and the cook and can see a bit of annoyance come over the cook's face. He proceeds to leave his work area bound for our table. I am watching the whole thing. As he made his way over, he engaged me. Right off the back, instead of asking how he could help, he said, "What's the problem?". As I wasn't expecting such a confrontation and was caught off guard, I was offended by his approach, tone and loudness, as if he was trying to bring attention from other customers to our table. I had to gather myself and keep a cool demeanor, because if it is anything I hate the most, it is being disrespected, especially in front of others. I bit my tongue and explained the simplicity of my situation to him. With a scolding tone, he rambles off on how the ordering works. Well, that was never the issue. The issue was about an additional food item that I ordered that the server wrote down that never came to our table. As the interaction seemed to intensify, I soon became aware and realized what was going on. This dude was trying to incite me, get me riled up and get me angry!

I am sure he was looking for a reason to call the police on me! This was a man-Karen! Once I realized the "set-up," from that point on, all I asked was to please bring me what I ordered. Mind you, the food did not come out until we were all practically done with our meals.

As a privileged White American, you will most likely always have a decent, if not excellent service experience. As a privileged White American, you have no idea of what it is like to be disrespected by restaurant employees and managers. Making ignorant stereotypical statements regarding the tipping habits of Black Americans is ridiculous, and if you claim yourself to be educated at the highest level, then you should be highly ashamed of yourselves for supporting such insensitive and shallow ways of thinking. As a Black American, I typically get decent service. Usually nothing special or over the top. On a few occasions I've received excellent service, but not more than the racist and bad service. I tip accordingly. I personally tip based on when I get decent service. When I get excellent service, I typically will tip beyond the highest percent. If I get a server who is rude, condescending, arrogant, acting like they are bothered because I speak up about something being forgotten that I ordered or asking a question about a menu item, then be sure that a less than favorable tip is on the way. And if the treatment I receive is so racially hostile, then I will not tip at all! It is all about treatment. If one is treated with dignity and respect, then that alone goes a long way when it comes to tipping. But hey, the non-black experts and radio talk show hosts seem to know better than the ones going through these experiences, as if we are too stupid to understand our own situations.

So, a message to all the Black Americans out there, especially the young ones: whenever a racist or someone is trying to come at you crazy and it sounds crazy and feels crazy, beware that it is most likely an attempt to get you caught up so they can label you as the crazy one! If the cops are called, most likely you will be kicked out of the establishment, especially if you have lost your cool by this time. I have seen similar things like this go down time and time again. Once I came to this realization, I let it go! I should have spoken to the manager, but because all this happened in earshot of the entire medium-sized restaurant, I am sure if a manager was on-site, he or she would have easily picked up on what was going on and would have intervened. I was done with the issue and wanted to enjoy the rest of my time with my family.

Not more than 58 years ago, my mother, growing up in a small East Texas town of Port Arthur, found herself in the wrong ice cream parlor on the wrong side of town. My mother, who doesn't cuss, doesn't drink and was a straight-A student, called my grandmother from jail as they had arrested her for local civil violations of a colored person in a white only restaurant. Whether my mom knew or not that she was in violation of this law, my point is that discrimination has its roots in the restaurant industry and still exists today in many different conspicuous manners.

"Within the U.S. restaurant industry, black customers are generally considered comparatively poor tippers. One recent survey of roughly 1,000 restaurant servers from across the nation found that 34 percent thought black diners were "very bad" tippers. An additional 36 percent thought black patrons were "below average" tippers. In contrast, 98 percent of those surveyed believed white customers were "average" or above average" tippers. Some readers may assume that such differences in tipping simply reflect widely documented differences in disposable income across the two groups. Given that tips are purported to reflect the quality of service that customers receive, others may argue that black patrons tend to tip less than their white counterparts because they are, on average, given comparatively inferior service" (Brewster, 2015).

In this last citing, yeah, of course the disparities in income compared from Black Americans to White Americans will prove as contributing factors to these tipping differences, but prejudices, racism and discrimination should be considered with perhaps greater significance. Also, and as the last citing suggests, ask yourself, who typically would have access to disposable income? I guarantee you that many more Black Americans do not have disposable income as do White Americans. Can anyone guess the root of this issue? For Black Americans, high unemployment and poverty rates and a lack of high-wage paying white-collar jobs will impact what a patron will give as a tip. "Black unemployment is at least twice as high as white unemployment at the national level. In the fourth quarter of 2018, African American workers had the highest unemployment rate nationally, at 6.5 percent, followed by Hispanic at 4.5 percent, Asian at 3.2 percent and white workers at 3.1 percent" (Wilson, 2019). "African Americans were worse off financially in 2016 than they were in 2000. The median income for an African American household was $39,490 last year, according to the U.S. Census Bureau. African Americans are the only racial group the Census Bureau identifies that has been left behind. White, Asian and Hispanic households have all seen at least modest income gains since 2000. Black Americans have struggled for years to move up the economic ladder, not to mention the difficulty in finding jobs and landing careers. Merely having an "African American sounding name" makes an employer less likely to hire someone, a National Bureau of Economic Research study found. The black unemployment rate is nearly double the white unemployment rate. It's been that way since the Labor Department began keeping track of unemployment by race in the early 1970s. "Black Americans also receive substantially lower wages than Whites and Asians" (Long, 2017). The census data report of 2016 showed that the median income for Black Americans was $39,490 and for White Americans, $69,041.

Take a moment to think about that. Black American unemployment rates are higher than White Americans and salary earnings for White Americans are much higher than that of Black Americans. Do these people who think Black Americans are poor tippers think it's just because they are being cheap or because they are black? Just like the rest of America's citizens, Whites, Asians, Hispanics, Indians, etc., we all like to go out to eat from time to time. It is what being an American is all about, regardless of income levels. Some just have different budgets. When you combine this and analyze the high cost in meals and poor service, then one should have the common sense understanding and knowledge as to why Black American patrons tip their servers the way they do. Unfortunately, it is just too easy and convenient for people to fall for the stereotypes, while others do not like their agendas to be tampered with. Remember, for the Black American, treatment may equal better tips, and if you happen to give excellent treatment, consider financial disparities compared to other groups. Ask yourself why such disparities among wage differences and unemployment rates exist. Maybe it has a bit to do with racism, discrimination and covert societal systemic oppression. Or perhaps the ideology of NGH is the common denominator. Income disparities and racist treatments are meaningless to those who make the Black American consumer tipping phenomenon such an issue and topic of their discussions. Let's just call it a classic case of ignorance!

PROPERTY

A few years ago, a close family member of mine was in the housing market looking to purchase a vacation home. I happen to be working in the real estate profession and she asked me if I could help find her a home. Before she contacted me, she had already paid a visit to the town in which she was interested in buying. She was ready to make a purchase in cash for whatever it was she liked. Initially, she went to the local real estate office where she was met with disrespect and hostility. However, she did not share this experience with me. It wasn't until we found a property she liked and made an offer that was accepted. The listing agent of the property stated she would like to talk to me about something. She proceeded to tell me, "You know, I felt really bad and embarrassed for your cousin when she came into our office. As I was seated in my office, I saw her come in and the office managers and another salesperson were the ones to greet her". She proceeded to tell me, "When your cousin came in, they treated her so unkind, they were rude and told her that they were too busy as they were pre-occupied with trying to fix the office copy machine. They told her to contact the office by phone later and make an appointment before coming in. They told her to come back once she had made an appointment". Here is the thing: you NEVER send a potential client away like that, especially without obtaining their information, and of course, you treat the customer with dignity and respect. In this case, none of that took place. At the time, I believe my cousin had forgotten I was a real estate agent. She went there unrepresented. Had the folks at that office realized that this would have been a double-ended deal for them in cash, they would have made a considerable commission as representatives for the listing and purchase. My cousin was obviously judged by the color of her skin and not as an individual. Either they were flat out racist and/or assumed that my cousin could not afford anything in the area and that she would have been a waste of time. Either way, they missed out on a huge commission!

Just like in all aspects of American life, full of racists, bigots and white supremacists, racism is alive in the business of property leasing and ownership. When my parents de-cided to move to South San Francisco, they had considered moving to Brisbane, which is situated between San Francis-co and South San Francisco towards the east. The real estate industry has a history of keeping Black Americans and other ethnic minorities out of certain communities throughout the US, which prevented my family from moving to this town. My mom recalls that the real estate folks in Brisbane were not at all helpful nor willing to assist them with their inquiries of available properties. Prior to my birth, when my mom and uncle first came to San Francisco, they were looking for an apartment to rent. As they approached an available rental, a white woman in an upper- level window of the apartment complex yelled out of the window, "We don't rent to Niggers". The allure of liberal attitudes and a sense of better opportunities for Black Americans is the reason many black families migrated from the southern states to places such as San Francisco and the greater Bay Area, but racism proved to be in existence even in one of the most socially acceptable regions in the United States.

In 2019, in Contra Costa County, a home buyer noticed on some of the property documents from the purchase of her home in Concord, California in 2010, that there was some discriminatory language. The document stated that the home could not be owned or occupied by anyone who was not of the Caucasian race.

"In the 1930s and 1940s, it was common practice for developers across the country to bar certain races from moving into their newly built homes, a discriminatory practice that also made its mark in the Bay Area. While those rules can no longer be enforced, they can't be entirely erased either, so they remain on the books in neighborhoods from the Oakland Hills to Redwood City and beyond. They're a rare but jarring reminder of the progressive region's painful history of discrimination. Such bans are usually found among the 'covenants, conditions, and restrictions' listed in a home's preliminary title report, which a buyer is asked to sign once his or her offer is accepted. A 1939 Redwood City home recently put up for sale, for example, includes a rule stating 'no person of any race other than the Caucasian or white race' may use or occupy the property, with the exception of domestic servants of a different race domiciled with an owner or tenant. Other covenants from that era specifically prohibit residents of 'African, Mongolian, or Japanese' descent. 'It was a very powerful disincentive for African-Americans to buy homes in white neighborhoods, because a white home owner who sold a home to an African American ran the risks of a lawsuit', said Richard Rothstein, an author of 'The Color of Law,' which explores the racial history of segregation. And those discriminatory rules were enforced. Rothstein's book tells the story of African-American physician DeWitt Buckingham, who bought a house in Berkeley's Claremont neighborhood from a white friend in 1945. A local neighborhood association sued, citing the covenant restricting the area to those of "pure Caucasian blood". (Kendall, 2019).

"African Americans bore the brunt of the federal and local exclusionary tactics, including steering by real estate agencies, racial covenants and federal housing policy. For example, the federal government created a segregated black housing project for black war workers in the Fillmore district, while white war workers were housed elsewhere in the city. By the 1970s, African Americans lived primarily in Oakland, Richmond, East Palo Alto, Pittsburg, Vallejo and designated neighborhoods in San Francisco, such as Bayview/Hunters Point. Richmond's Iron Triangle, East Oakland, West Oakland and Bayview/Hunters Point were regional examples of inner-city neighborhoods starved of resources and then hemmed in by racial housing policies" (Gambhir, 2019).

Ways in which racists tried preventing people of color from moving into their neighborhoods were often a matter of life and death!

"Several lynching's in the Bay Area were documented, although information on the full extent is incomplete. Historian Monroe Nathan Work (1866-1945), who meticulously recorded lynching's across the country as part of his work at the Tuskegee Institute, documented three acts of white supremacist lynching's in the Bay Area between 1880 and 1920. These murders were carried out against a Black man in San Jose in 1892, a Mexican Man in Los Gatos in 1883 and another Mexican man in Santa Rosa in 1920.

A Chinese family in the 1950s found a house in a subdivision of South San Francisco and purchased their home for $12,300. When white neighbors learned that a Chinese American family was moving in, the white neighbors protested. The new Chinese American home-owner Mr. Sheng was confronted by 75 white homeowners as he attended a local neighborhood meeting where these white home-owners expressed opposition to his family moving into their neighborhood. The white neighbors were concerned that their property values would decrease, although they expressed that they had no personal bad feelings towards Mr. Sheng.

The Gentrification and displacement happening in the San Francisco Bay Area today may seem far removed from the blatant racial discrimination that the Shengs faced in the 1950s, but these stories are deeply connected. While the booming tech sector, globalized finance and other forces shaping housing in the region are new, racial exclusion in housing is not. The region's past and present are both stories of a system of racial capitalism, in which race and racism are fundamental to the creation of profit and accumulation of wealth.

The rampant displacement seen today in the San Francisco Bay Area is built upon a history of exclusion and dispossession, centered on race and driven by the logic of capitalism. This history established massive inequities in who owned land, who had access to financing and who held political power, all of which determined, and still remain at the root of deciding, who can call the Bay Area home" (Eli Moore, 2019).

AFFIRMATIVE ACTION

For those who are not familiar with Affirmative Action, this was a law policy adopted by several states that prevented businesses, companies, employers and educational institutions from discrimination based on race, religion, creed and national origin. This law was put in place with the goal of ensuring fair and equal access to these public entities by promoting more diversity as historical events proved the lack thereof.

Founder and Chairman of the American Civil Rights Institute and President of the Californians for Equal Rights, Ward Connerly, a successful Black American businessman, helped lead the campaign in abolishing Affirmative Action under California Law Proposition 209 (the California Civil Rights Initiative) in 1996. This law eliminated the requirements from employers and educational institutions from considering race and ethnicity in their hiring and enrollment practices. One of the noted reasons for its abolishment was that "apparently", research data showed that White and

Asian students were being denied admission into colleges despite having better grades and academic scores than other students that were being admitted. This allowed universities to consider social and economic factors instead. Just think about that for a minute.

I mean, this shit actually sounds dumb ASF! I'm not going to dig deep into this, but damn! Black Americans have always had low admission rates into colleges. Black Americans' median incomes here in the United States have always been much lower than White and Asian Americans and I am sure these educational institutions were not in any hurry to consider admissions from low-income applicants or applicants coming from "urban" backgrounds! From my observations, it seems to me that there has been no difference either way, but at least with such a law, the opportunity was there to help and assist those who are discriminated against in order to make things more possible and equitable. If sound enforcement and assurances took place for the utilization of the law, perhaps there would have been more Black Americans on college campuses. It is often hard to believe that there are black politicians who support thinking along these lines. It is disappointing that a black "civil rights" leader accepted this! I had a very hard fucking time trying to find work in the 90s! Application after application and not one callback! And at this time, while seeking gainful employment, Affirmative Action was still in place!

However, this abolishment just made it that much harder for Black Americans to find employment. Although things were difficult (and like I mentioned before, I wasn't going to take the easy way out), the alternative seemed quite tempting! The main reason I didn't was due to low-life expectancy, and I couldn't see voluntarily handing my life over to a system that was originally designed to oppress Black Americans through this avenue of systemic racism. Nevertheless, I imagine that I was screened out of these jobs when I honestly checked the Black/African American ethnicity box on those employment applications! Not only was I more than qualified for a simple job working as a grocery clerk, but I also couldn't even get a damn interview from any of the multiple local grocery stores I had applied to in the region.

My cousin was a UC Davis graduate back in the 90s. While attending school there he invited me to several functions. While on campus at these various functions, I did not see any other Black American students. During visits with my son, who recently graduated from UC Davis in 2019, on numerous occasions I could probably count on one hand how many Black American students I saw amongst the thousands of students. The majority of the students I observed were Whites and Asians. However, I did see Black Americans during the African American graduation celebration and at the African American family day, but these were isolated events. On a regular school day, you'd rarely see a black face. In the year 2000, it was reported that only 2.7 percent of undergraduate students at UC Davis were Black Americans, and almost 20 years later, only 3.0 percent were Black Americans. And you tell me that Whites and Asians were being denied admissions? Absolutely laughable! All the work that prior civil rights leaders fought for was being dismantled here in California by a man noted as a "Civil Rights" leader. Only in America. Talk about feeling defeated as a Black American! Some folks believe that Affirmative Action demeans the Black American community. The thinking behind that is that Black Americans need "special assistance." The day racism, hate and discrimination are 100 percent eradicated from America, then I can guarantee you special assistance is not needed. But then many of you, including a few Black Americans, believe there is no racism. On the contrary, assistance is needed as long as systemic oppression is alive and well, for the well-being of all citizens in America.

THE MEDIA

The media has played a huge part in shaping the opinions and thoughts of American citizens towards Black Americans for hundreds of years. History shows that Black Americans were the targets of negative ideologies based on offensive and dehumanizing stereotypes. "Time and time again, powerful and brilliant men and women have produced racist ideas in order to justify the racist policies of their era. Arguably, the most racial policy of any era was the one that allowed whites in this country to call black people property-chattel during slavery" (Costello/Douez, 2017). The media's role in shaping the opinions and thoughts of Americans goes as far back as slavery and, most importantly, during the onset of slaves being freed. This would forever remain as a major obstacle and set-back to equality and freedom for Black Americans generation after generation.

"One of the most enduring stereotypes in American history is that of the Sambo. This pervasive image of a simple-minded, docile black man dates back at least as far as the colonization of America. The Sambo stereotype flourished during the reign of slavery in the United States. In fact, the notion of the "happy slave" is the core of the Sambo caricature. White slave owners molded African-American males, as a whole, into this image of a jolly, overgrown child who was happy to serve his master. However, the Sambo was seen as naturally lazy and therefore reliant upon his master for direction. In this way, the institution of slavery was justified. Bishop Wipple's Southern Diary, 1834-1844, is evidence of this justification of slavery, 'They seem a happy race of beings and if you did not know it you would never imagine that they were slaves.' It is essential to realize the vast scope of this stereotype. It was transmitted through music titles and lyrics, folk sayings, literature, children's stories and games, postcards, restaurant names and menus and thousands of artifacts. White women, men and children across the country embraced the image of the fat, wide- eyed, grinning black man. It was perpetuated over and over, shaping enduring attitudes toward African-Americans for centuries. In fact, a stereotype may be so consistently and authoritatively transmitted in each generation from parent to child that it seems almost biological in fact" (Boskin, 1986).

For the last 20 to 30 years, daytime TV talk shows and judge shows should be viewed as such participators in the continuance and supporters of modern-day stereotypes, which proves as a direct lineage of the stereotypes used as far back as slavery times. "One reason racism persists into contemporary times is because racist ideas are passed down from one generation to the next. Hearing generalizations, even positive or neutral ones, contributes to the tendency to view the world through the lens of social stereotypes" (Douez & Costello, 2017). These present-day TV shows exploit Black Americans as dysfunctional, un-educated, animated, loud and obnoxious. Black American participants who fall for the "one minute of fame" are actually confirming and solidifying the present-day negative stereotypes and images as absolute truths while continuously tarnishing the Black American image amongst the naive, the innocent, the ignorant, the guiltless and the racist. Although some portray themselves in these stereotypical ways, it is important to know that there are many more Black Americans who do not act in or behave in such a manner. It is also important to know that other races of people, including whites, act and behave in the same exact ways as the negative stereotypes attributed to Black Americans. "Perhaps the most discussed pattern is the association between black males and criminality, particularly in television news, where they are not only to appear as criminals, but likely to be shown in ways that make them seem particularly threatening" (The Opportunity Agenda, 2004). Unfortunately, and in my opinion, this is part of a systemic tactic of attacks against Black Americans for justifying the whole ideology behind NGH.

"For various reasons, media of all types collectively offer a distorted representation of the lives and reality of black males. In turn, media consumption negatively affects the public's understandings related to black males (sometimes including the understandings and attitudes of black males themselves). Finally, these distorted understandings and attitudes towards black males lead to negative real-world consequences for them. The distorted images in the media make it easier for many Americans to tolerate, perpetuate, ignore or discount the many real disadvantages that black males face. For example, although characters of color in video games have been increasing over time, blacks in general tend to be underrepresented especially as active, playable characters in video games. They are more likely to be stock characters in the story... outside of sports games, the representation of African Americans [in popular video games] drops precipitously, with many of the remaining featured as gangsters and street people. Black men [in mainstream print ads], with rare exceptions, are represented as workers, athletes, laborers, entertainers, criminals, or some combination thereof" (The Opportunity Agenda, 2004).

As in the example of the Facebook post mentioned earlier, it seems many folks do not really understand Black Lives Matter (BLM) or really understand Black American lives at all. They rely on and trust the media and politicians to shape their views, attitudes and beliefs, therefore taking what they see and hear at face value. People who rely on and believe everything they see and hear in the media often fall victim to the stereotypical rhetoric and end up getting misinformed about the intent and truthfulness about organized groups such as BLM. Many folks will believe that BLM is a radical extremist or terrorist group and not a group that organized in solidarity to address the acts of terrorism brought against Black Americans. If you do the research of black historical movements in this country, you will begin to see a common thread and start to take notice of who the real extremists and terrorists are. The media has been used to instill fear into White American citizens of organized black movements and used to discredit these movements by labeling these movements as extremist, radical organizations. When I think of an extremist, the first thing that comes to my mind due to American media, is middle eastern radical groups classified as terrorist organizations by the American Government. The labeling of Black American organizations as extremists under the perceptions of mainstream America is outright dangerous!

It is very common that many folks tend to believe everything coming from the media in all its forms and the America's political leaders. These sources will have you believe that these Black American movements are dangerous and violent, resulting in cutting off the potential for any support from others that are necessary for societal change and the betterment for all people. "To deflect legitimate criticism of police tactics, to undermine a legitimate protest movement that has emerged in the past three years to protest police brutality, the FBI has tarred the dissenters as domestic terrorists, an organized group with a criminal ideology that is a threat to police officers. Whenever you create an assumption that somebody possesses a physical threat to law enforcement, that provides incentive for law enforcement to shoot first and ask questions later. Further, and should cause great concern to all citizens of America, when the report was leaked to Foreign Policy later in 2017, it prompted fierce and widespread criticism from activists, civil right advocates, and lawmakers, many of whom accused the FBI of reverting to the surveillance and sabotage of black activists that had defined its activities in the civil rights era" (Speri, 2019).

Such intent by high-status law enforcement agencies such as the FBI, is a prime example of not only disrupting and shutting down a legitimate movement, but also putting these protestors in harm's way of white extremists for retaliatory violence. An example is the White American woman in Charlottesville, Heather Heyer, who in 2017 was murdered by a white supremacist as he intentionally drove his car into a crowd of peaceful counter-protestors. On August 25, 2020, a young white man named Jacob Blake brought a long-rifle to a protest following another shooting of an unarmed Black American in Wisconsin. The gunman reportedly was there to help quell "looters" from further property destruction. The man ended up shooting down and killing two people and shooting the arm off another at the protest as they attempted to disarm the young man. This man actually shot these men down in front of protestors, including the police. The police did nothing and let this man continue to walk the streets and was only arrested hours later at his home. Is this a direct result of Trump, his campaign and supporters who have been instilling fear into White Americans during the presidential campaign, touting their followers to believe that anarchists, rioters and looters will find their way to the suburbs with the potential to cause harm to white folks?

Dr. Martin Luther King, Jr., the most prolific, notable and peaceful non-violent protester of his time, was also deemed an extremist by White America. However, Dr. King's response to the labeling as an extremist was that "he found pride" in being called an extremist. He argued that extremism only means extreme devotion to a cause and provided several examples of unimpeachable figures who showed extremism, such as Jesus, an extremist for love" (Cedars, 2014). I totally see Dr. King's point of view on being labeled an extremist. However, the problem with America is that when the label of an extremist is given to a person or a group by the ones in political control and power, it is used to denote a negative ideology with criminal intentions and the person or group targeted by such labeling tactics is automatically viewed as the enemy or a threat to the greater American society. According to Dictionary.com, the definition of extremist is "a person who goes to extremes, especially in political matters, a supporter or advocate of extreme doctrines or practice". Wikipedia defines extremism as "the quality or state of being extreme" or "the advocacy of extreme measures or views". "Political agendas perceived as extremist often include those from the far-left politics or far-right politics as well as radicalism, reactionism, fundamentalism and fanaticism". These definitions provide clear meaning, however, the way the meaning is used in America comes with a twist. The twist of truth, from which being an extremist in a quest and demand for equality, justice and fair treatment is turned into an extremist movement meant to attack, pillage, riot and destroy. Therefore, the intent of the movement is successfully devalued and demonized. And because of this twist, you will see a rise in attacks against minorities all over America.

For folks that just don't get it, this is why BLM exists. This organization did not come into existence with the perception that "only" black lives matter! The title, name, statement or phrase, as it is presented, are words of inclusion meant to pronounce and demand equality for Black Americans and all Americans. It is too bad that this calls for an explanation, and even worse, it is too bad that movements like BLM exist at all. It is a telling feature of the truth about the real "Great America". If we all have some sense of morality, we all know that all lives matter. However, many Black Americans have lived in this society knowing that their lives do not matter and never have mattered based on a long, long history of oppression, hatred and unjust treatment. I do not understand why some folks need to say, "blue lives matter" or that "white lives matter". As a police officer, of course their lives matter. However, their profession comes with a high risk, the risk of being killed in the line of duty. Police officers understand this. Those who are sworn in and whose job it is to arrest rapists and murderers or those facing life-sentences know that these criminals most likely don't want to be imprisoned for the rest of their lives, so they may try to kill those that need to apprehend them. So, in my opinion, it sounds outright ridiculous to say, "blue lives matter."

A murderous criminal on the run does not give a shit about a life. Is that who the slogan "blue lives matter" is meant for, for the criminal? I am sure law-abiding citizens already understand that police officer's lives matter. And furthermore, as a white person, you should know that your life matters. It has always mattered! It does not have to be said and it comes with being white in America. You don't have to demand it; you don't have to express it and it is a given fact of American culture. It is so interesting to see the passion in some folks making these outrageous statements. You almost wonder if these people have some sort of cognitive disability hindering their ability to decipher the differences or acknowledge the realities of American life for minorities versus non-minorities. Yes, all lives matter, but due to the mistreatment of Black Americans, from slavery to Jim Crow, to disease experimentation, segregation, to employment and housing discrimination and as everyday consumers, Black Americans have faced huge adversities navigating their lives through a racist system. Black Americans only want the world to wake up and realize that we matter just like any other life and the lives of other non-blacks. Black Americans only want to be given equal rights, just like the equal rights that should be given to all citizens of America. Black Americans have always had to demand equality and freedom in a society controlled and manipulated by those in power, who are often racist themselves, those who do not believe racism exists, and those who have no empathy for the Black American experience.

People need to understand and remember that "The media world is populated by some black males we admire, but these tend to be associated with a relatively limited range of qualities, such as physical ability and/or entertainment skills. In the entertainment media as well, these and other associations continue to be systematically perpetuated. Analysts have gone into great detail about the way in which negative images of black males continue to be used for entertainment purposes, whether through traditional imagery of black inferiority or by using black male characters to represent both the victims and perpetrators of violence. Without being conscious of biased attitudes, producers of media content of all kinds may, consciously or unconsciously, assume that people with low incomes tend to be black, or looking at this another way, that households with black males are likely to be dysfunctional, that discrimination against black males is limited to isolated acts of racial discrimination, and so on" (The Opportunity Agenda, 2004).

The only Black Americans that seem to get around this are those who are rich, famous and well known by society. If you are not, you will be subjected to daily rituals of racism no matter if you are a poor black, middle-class black or wealthy black. There is no difference between the ones who fall for the stereotypes and America's racists. When you have the President saying things like Mexicans are rapists, then you will undoubtedly have small-minded people who fall for the rhetoric, thus putting all Mexicans at risk for some sort of racial attack. In "The Hate Behind the Attack", the gunman had allegedly driven more than 600 miles across the state from North Texas to target Hispanics in the border community. The shooting at Walmart took place due to the merging of three systemic problems, said Garcia, "gun access, white supremacy and the President's anti-immigrant rhetoric" (Dearman, 2020). Apparently, this young white supremacist felt that Mexicans were invading America, and on August 3, 2019, he made the long trip to El Paso to a local Walmart where he carried out the shooting targeting Hispanics, which left 22 people dead.

One thing is clear: in America you never hear anything about common white criminals. It's as if they do not exist, especially in the media. You definitely will never hear anyone saying "white-on-white" crime, even though most crimes committed against people by whites are against other whites. White people commit the same crimes as any other ethnic group, from petty crimes to serious and violent crimes such as murder. American citizens need to stop falling for the rhetoric regarding the criminalization of Black and Mexican Americans and think deeper, especially when it comes to race perceptions in right-wing politics and the stereotypes portrayed and fueled by the media. Despite all the injustices dating back for centuries, Black Americans continue to create successful lives for themselves by far surpassing the number of criminals. Average, everyday common Black American success is not newsworthy to the media. What makes the news is what feeds into the stereotypical views. The majority of Black Americans are not criminals! The census data reports just over two million Black Americans in California, and incarceration data reports of Black Americans as of May 2020 is a bit over 50 thousand. This number is high compared to incarceration rates of other non-black Californians, but this phenomenon, a totally different subject, needs extreme in-depth analysis of the history of the American penal system relating to Black Americans for people to begin to understand the truth behind the high incarceration rates. My point is only to show that two million Black Californians compared to 50 thousand proves that not all Black Americans are criminals. For the non-black and non-white communities that may have unfortunately fell victim to "black crime", do not let the media and a small percentage of the criminal element shape your mind into believing all Black Americans are bad people. Do not allow yourselves to become racist because of what you see and hear.

The media and some politicians will continue to focus on Black Americans as bad people. That is their agenda. There is bad in every group of people and it's unfortunate that America is more concerned with exploiting the Black American on this stage. All ethnic groups need to understand and realize that we all come from oppressed backgrounds imposed by the "ones in charge". I find it very unsettling for Black, Latino, Middle Eastern, Asian and other non-white Americans to be racist towards one another. What that suggests is that these people have accepted racial stereotypes as truths and have fallen victim to negative attitudes and perceptions inflicted upon them without thought. What makes this even worse is that some are even clueless to their very own state of consciousness regarding their adopted racist perceptions or how it came about in the first place. Minorities of all ethnic backgrounds need to understand that we all share a common thread. During the civil rights era, Black Americans fought for equality and all minority cultures here in America directly benefited. If the racist leaders of today had their way, we would all be returned to concentration camps, slavery or deported. The racist "forefathers" made a huge mistake, and that was to bring in ethnic minority groups to America to shape and build its infrastructure. Now it seems that their descendants are going crazy! The United States is a multicultural country and all who are here are here to stay. Racism has no place in this country! Black America is America. Asian America is America. Mexican America is America. White America is America and America is home to all of us.

America should look past ethnicity and call crime what it is, a "crime". Not black-on-black crime, but crime. Ethnic political leaders should make it a point to denounce all efforts to attribute crime to particular racial groups and instead put energy into promoting cultural diversity by exploiting the good in all people and rejecting the bad. If you ran for office to serve any community in this country, then representation should focus on the community as a whole, bringing ALL people together and inviting and encouraging diverse cultures to share in their celebrations, rituals, fairs and ceremonies. Without that, there will always be division, racism and hate in this country. Hate cannot prevail, yet it could potentially take us all out!

Citizens of America should beware of the stereotypes that the media and some politician's support. They should think beyond the stereotypes that have suffocated this nation and have brought out the ugly in people. These stereotypes keep this country divided, not just with the Black American, but with many minority Americans. Citizens should help out their fellow man and woman, their fellow neighbor, regardless of the color of his/her skin. America is not united and never has been. Let's now unite! The negative in one race is not exclusive to that race. Whites, Latins, Asians, Blacks, Natives, Middle Easterners, etc. are all human. Unfortunately, you will find the bad in all humans. Caution yourselves to assigning negative behaviors to one group of people based on their race. Statisticians, and folks who immerse themselves with statistics based on ethnic background and race, are not really concerned with the root of why some ethnic groups tend to show higher rates of whatever their focus of studies happens to be, especially when it comes to the depraved and negative behavior of certain groups. Unless America becomes a country that truly offers equality to all from birth to death, the racist statistics reflecting negative behavior should be dismissed. If not, then the whole NGH ideology will thrive throughout this country, not only affecting Black Americans but affecting all minorities of America.

FAMILY AND FRIENDS

I wrote this book because I wanted to share the experiences I have had as a Black American living in a society that has its roots intertwined with decades and decades of mistreatment and discrimination. The phrase NGH was my initiation into a society sickened with hate. These were my experiences. I am sure thousands of others have similar ones, as well as very different stories. Close family and friends of mine have their own stories and I wanted to share with the reader some of their stories as well.

I find it interesting that many of my elders, mainly the generation before me which included parents, aunts and uncles, shared a commonality in regard to racist experiences. That commonality was that they could not recall many experiences. I wondered how this could be as they were all from southern states (Louisiana and Texas) known for white supremacy, hate and racism. I quickly learned that it wasn't because racism did not exist for them, but because they all lived in a segregated south with very minimal contact with whites. Back in those days, folks had to work hard labor jobs. My father and uncle explained to me, that as early as seven years old, they recall working long hours. My uncle stated he had to drop out of middle school to help out the family. Both my uncle and father reported that they grew up with no running water, makeshift out-houses to use as bathrooms and would have to go to local gas stations or wells to fill up huge water containers for their daily water needs for cooking, bathing and washing. They worked the fields, helped raise farm animals and tended to the crops. Their youthful days were spent doing endless chores or trying to earn money. They reported they were too busy working all day every day in their segregated towns, mostly unexposed to racial issues outside of their neighborhoods, to reflect and think about racial relations. However, they did have some stories to tell.

FRIEND ACCOUNTS

One of my best friends, a Black American who is like a brother to me, lived around the corner from me where we grew up. In that house, he had an encounter with the police where guns were drawn. I believe we were in our first or second year of high school and his family had just rented a room to a White woman in order to help his mom make ends meet. One late night or early morning, my friend gets hungry and decides to get some food in the kitchen. Apparently, the roommate heard movement and the dogs outside barking, so she called the police without informing anyone else in the house. Two police officers had made entry into their home, and with guns drawn, confronted my friend in the dark in his kitchen while standing in his underwear holding a hot dog. Thank God they did not mistake the hotdog for a weapon! Why would the police make entry into a home, guns drawn, and not be aware that an entire family was living in the house? This could have ended in tragedy! I wonder if there was any prior knowledge of the racial make-up of the occupants inside the house. Something just did not seem quite right in that situation.

My same friend, some years later and now living on his own, was renting an apartment in Mountain View, California. He was working for a tech company at the beginning of the Silicon Valley tech boom. As a tenant of this complex, he stated he was often harassed by a white woman who was the apartment manager. She was known to make racial comments and slurs to him and told him he needed to be living in East Palo Alto, a predominately Black and Hispanic neighborhood in the Bay Area.

One summer day, my Black American friend was with one of our close friends. He's a White American who is down to earth, logical in his thinking and also like a brother to me. They were going to Redwood City to visit with family. During this time, we were all in middle school. My white friend had an uncle and aunt that lived there. My friends told me about their experience with racism after visiting with his aunt. On their way to the bus stop to head home they had stopped by a local store. While at the store, an older white male says to them, "Look, it's a Nigger". From that point, a confrontation took place and my Black American friend ended up knocking this older guy out! Luckily, the racist guy didn't have a weapon. You just never know what these terrorists have up their sleeves. Just another NGH moment in time!

MOMS

Moms had a couple of interesting things to say about being arrested alongside her friends in her hometown in Texas for being on the wrong side of town in an ice cream parlor when she was a teenager. She also told me that there was a derogatory term besides Nigger that white folks used to describe Black American men that I have never heard. That was the term "Rastus". Rastus has been used as a generic, often derogatory name for black men since at least 1880 (Wikipedia). Moms recalls the days of seeing drinking fountains labeled for whites and colored. In addition, she recalls going shoe shopping with her mom. During her time as a little girl, blacks were not allowed to try on shoes or measure their feet and often were not allowed in the shoe stores at all. My grandmother would have to trace and outline their feet on paper or cardboard and bring her cut-out tracing to the shoe store. Because grandma was white and my mother mixed, moms would be identified as black and therefore denied services and/or entry. My grandmother's tracings in those situations came in handy.

STEP-FATHER

My step-father, a professional and very accomplished businessman, currently runs and operates his own successful tax and bookkeeping business and has for the past 30 years. He previously held a high position with the local Pacific Bell telephone company, while simultaneously operating his own trophy shop in San Francisco near the Cow Palace. He had hired me for a summertime position and taught me how to make trophies before he started to date my mom. I was intrigued and curious by the success of my step-father as a professional Black American and looked up to him as a positive force and role model. I was surprised to learn one of his stories, which had taken place in the 1950s. He had just graduated from tech school after completing basic training in the United States Air Force and was on his way to his permanent base in Abilene, Texas, from St. Louis, Missouri (fig. 3). My step-father seemed to do everything by the "book," with an impressionable calm demeanor. He loved to tune into the San Francisco Giants baseball games on the radio as well as the San Francisco news station on KGO. Very serious about life, he would always tell my brothers and I that in order to become successful, "you've got to handle your business". I took that phrase as a message to keep going to school, get a higher- education and find a career in order to sustain our lives.

Figure 3 1958-Stepfather-United States Air Force

Educated, successful, intelligent and as responsible as my step-father was, as a young black man he would be met with a smack of racism and hate as a reminder of what it was like to be young and black and living in America during the 50s and 60s. A friend of my step-father from basic training happened to have a car and convinced my step-father to ride with him to his home town in Jackson, Mississippi. He did not want to make the trip alone. Once in Mississippi, he would drop my step-father off at the Trailways bus station in order to continue his trip to Texas. He got his ticket and made his way onto the bus, taking a seat in the third or fourth row from the front. It was December 5, 1958, when he arrived in Tula, Louisiana. The bus driver told him as they pulled into a rest area "boy, the law is going to get you". My stepfather replied back, that according to federal law, you can sit wherever you want on the bus while on interstate travel. Fearing trouble would follow, my step-father contacted the FBI on the payphone while at the rest stop. The FBI confirmed that he could in fact sit wherever he wanted on the bus as an interstate passenger. My step-father got back on the bus, and within a few minutes, a sheriff's deputy ordered him to get from the bus. My step-father explains his rights and that he is a military person serving in the United States Air Force. He was still placed in handcuffs and taken to jail (just like Rosa Parks three years prior in Montgomery, Alabama, December of 1955) for taking a seat on the front of the bus. See figure 4 court document which states, "did insist upon going into a seat designated for the white race on the Trailways Bus, he being of the colored race....". He would face two charges: Separate Accommodations for colored and Whites R.S. 45:194.5 and Refusal to Comply R.S. 45:195(see figure 5 arrest report).

Once jailed, my step-father was fingerprinted. When he asked about making his one phone call, the Deputy said to him, "Sign the document, Nigger". My step-father would serve the minimum term for the law violation, which was ten days. However, he had written a note to the FBI on a piece of toilet paper that explained his dilemma and handed the note to a jail-mate who was being released. He promised to mail it to the FBI. The FBI did get the note, however my step-father had served his time and had since made it to the Air Force base in Texas, where he was told to fill out a report regarding the incident.

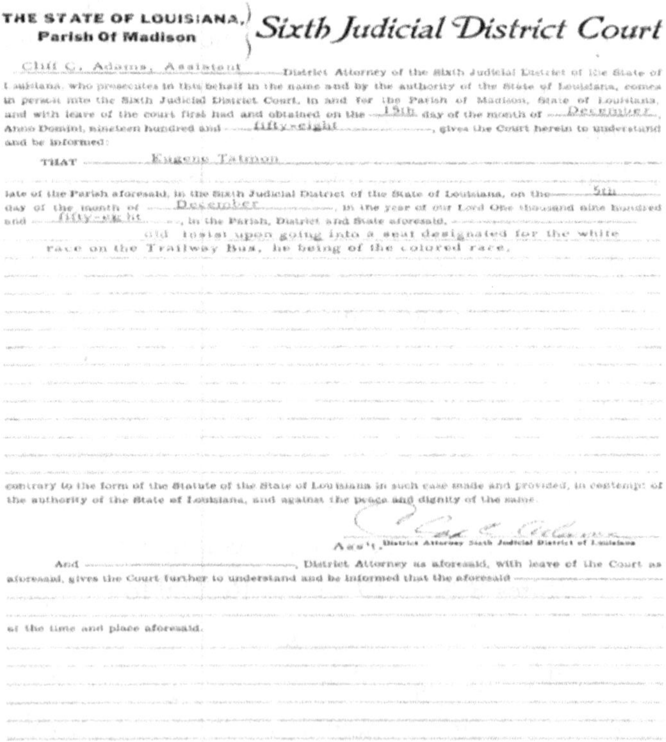

THE STATE OF LOUISIANA, Parish Of Madison } Sixth Judicial District Court

Cliff C. Adams, Assistant District Attorney of the Sixth Judicial District of the State of Louisiana, who prosecutes in this behalf in the name and by the authority of the State of Louisiana, comes in person into the Sixth Judicial District Court, in and for the Parish of Madison, State of Louisiana, and with leave of the court first had and obtained on the 15th day of the month of December, Anno Domini, nineteen hundred and fifty-eight, gives the Court herein to understand and be informed:

THAT Eugene Tatmon

late of the Parish aforesaid, in the Sixth Judicial District of the State of Louisiana, on the 5th day of the month of December, in the year of our Lord One thousand nine hundred and fifty-eight, in the Parish, District and State aforesaid,

did insist upon going into a seat designated for the white race on the Trailway Bus, he being of the colored race,

contrary to the form of the Statute of the State of Louisiana in such case made and provided, in contempt of the authority of the State of Louisiana, and against the peace and dignity of the same.

Ass't. District Attorney Sixth Judicial District of Louisiana

And ______, District Attorney as aforesaid, with leave of the Court as aforesaid, gives the Court further to understand and be informed that the aforesaid

at the time and place aforesaid.

Figure 4 Parish of Madison-court Criminal Affidavit

My step-father went on to receive an honorable discharge from the Air Force and later became the President of the California Jaycees, where he had the opportunity to meet then American President, Gerald Ford (fig. 6). He stated he had the opportunity to become a political official. However, he had no interest in politics because of the "politics".

Madison Parish Sheriff's Department

REPORT OF ARREST

12/5/58

Last Name	First Name		Alias		Arrest No.
TATMON, Eugene					143

Residence				Employer	
357 Center St., Oakland, Calif.				US Air Force	

Sex	Color	Age	Height	Weight	Hair	Eyes	Complexion	Occupation
M Male	Negro	13	5-9½	170	Blk	Brn	Lt. Bro.	US Air Force

Scars and Marks		Place of Birth	Date of Birth
Scar under right eye		Oakland, Calif.	1/24/40

Date of Arrest		Place of Arrest	
12/5/58		Tallulah, La.	

Charge		Complainant	
Vio. La. RS 45:194 & 195		R. R. Mitchell	

FACTS OF ARREST

Above subject was riding in white section of a Trailway Bus. He was seated in the third seat from the front when the bus arrived at the station here. Deputy Mitchell saw subject and asked him to move to the rear of the bus, which he refused to do. He was removed from the bus by Deputies Mitchell and Lott, and at their request, was given a transfer by the Bus Driver. He was placed in the Madison Parish Jail and charged with Violation of La. Statutes RS 45:194 (Seperate accomodations for white and colored) & RS 45:195 (Refusal to comply).

R. R. Mitchell & T. J. Lott

Arresting Officer

Prisoner	Address
Mitchell & Lott	

Signature	Address

Figure 5 Louisiana, Madison Parish-Arrest Report

A handshake between California Jaycee State President Gene Tatmon and President Gerald R. Ford on the occasion of the recent Jaycee Governmental Affairs Leadership Seminar

Figure 6 Stepfather meets the 38th United States President Gerald Ford, as President of the California Jaycees.

POPS

My father, whom my siblings and I refer to as "Pops", was born in the early 1940s in Crowley, Louisiana. He lived there until his early teens, prior to coming to California, and recalls a couple of racial incidents. Pops was a very hard worker and never got into any trouble. His work ethic and determination went unnoticed and his passion for sports was undeniable. There were no jobs for Black Americans in his small town in Louisiana, other than working as servants for white folks. As early as he could remember, around seven or eight years of age (fig. 7) and the youngest of labored cotton pickers, he recalls the trips to the cotton fields.

He stated that between 3:00 to 3:30 in the morning, the black folks in his neighborhood wanting to earn money would stand in front of their homes (which were about 100 to 400 yards apart) and would wait for white folks to drive through picking them up in their pick-up trucks and taking them to the fields to pick cotton for the day. Pops stated that they would ride in the back of the pick-up trucks standing straight up, as they were packed in like sardines. Being the smallest of all the workers, he recalls being squished in between the adults and being very tired most of the time, often falling asleep standing up on these truck rides to and from the cotton fields. My Pop's cousins were also among these field workers, and he recalls that one of his cousins was really good and fast at picking cotton. However, he didn't pick the cotton "clean". Pops said they would usually be paid at the end of their day and that they would have large sacks that were put on scales with hooks. They would then be "paid" according to the weight. Pops said it was typical for the whites to tamper with the scales and that they would often be cheated and shortchanged of their earnings. He said sometimes they wouldn't even pay you at all. It just depended on how they were feeling that day.

Figure 7 Pops-age 7 or 8

Water moccasin snakes and huge wasps were camou-
flaged among cotton plants as they worked the fields and
Pops said you had to be really careful in order to avoid getting bit or stung. To make matters worse, they would often
be intimidated by whites into picking cotton faster for more
product, rather than allowing the workers to pick cautiously.
Imagine you are working early morning hours, well into the
hot sun, trying to avoid dangerous snakes and wasps and
at the end of the day you may not even get paid! These
white cotton field landowners must have felt that these

171

field workers were unworthy of pay and that their health and safety did not matter. Sounds familiar! A human being working all day through the Louisiana hot sun, sweating and getting cut-up by cotton plant thorns while facing additional dangers, is worthy of payment and accommodation. But with the mindset of the confederation, there's no chance in hell! This sort of dehumanizing experience is one of so many situations that would manifest itself in the whole NGH ideology. The lives of Black Americans did not matter! Pops would always say, out of frustration of being underpaid or not paid at all, that he would often alter the bags prior to weigh-in, making them heavier in order to recoup his losses whenever white field owners felt like not being "fair".

Pops also recalls working for two white families on their plantations, the Cassidys and the Bunkers. Pops stated that he was never allowed to enter the Cassidy's home but would often be invited inside the Bunker's home by the Black American maid who would feed him lunch. Pops said he did landscape work such as mowing lawns, trimming hedges and pulling weeds. During those early days, there were no motorized lawn mowers or power tools. All tools were manual, and the yards were enormous! He would also do laundry at a time when there were no dryers. Whenever Pops wasn't working, he was hanging out with his two cousins. He says he really enjoyed the blackberry pie that his grandmother would make. His favorite cousin and he would go out to pick the blackberries that his grandmother would use in her pies. One day they were out picking blackberries and had followed this particular row of blackberry bushes to a point where they had to climb a fence to continue picking. While on the other side of the fence, they did not realize they were on someone's property. As they continued picking, they heard someone yelling out at them. And then they heard gunshots! They soon realized that this white man was yelling Niggers at them and for them to get off his land, while running and shooting his rifle in their direction. Pops said they ran and got away without being hurt! So, you ask yourself, why a gun? Why shoot at two young boys out picking blackberries? Did this man feel justified based on stereotypical and propaganda laden media reports during this time? I would guess most likely so. Did the man just have a pure hatred for Black Americans? Probably. Had he shot and killed my father and his cousin, I am sure the man would have been justified! You see, this has always been America.

Survival was tough and Pops and his family had to supplement their low wages by raising cows, chickens and growing their own crops in order to eat and sustain themselves. He stated they would often trade various fruits and vegetables with other local black families. He also mentioned that the clothes he wore were mainly hand-me-downs from white kids who lived on the plantations where he worked.

Pops said he went to a Catholic school and that you had to recite your catechism assignments. If you couldn't memorize and recite your assignments, such as the ten commandments, you would be smacked on the hands and knuckles by the white nuns. Once again sounding familiar! He also noted that because his hometown was growing with more and more Black Americans, they started to attend local white schools (prior to integration), but as soon as black students started showing up, all the whites kids started to be pulled from these schools. The poor whites living close to the blacks started moving out of their neighborhoods as the black population continued to expand.

While living in the South, Pops recalls how he was watched when entering stores, how bus stations had separate amenities for blacks and whites, and how most restaurants did not allow blacks. If you were riding the bus and it was full, you had to stand up to allow whites to sit, even while riding in the back. A few ice cream parlors that were open to blacks had a rule that blacks had to enter through the back entrance rather than the front.

At the age of fifteen, Pops moved to San Francisco to be with his mom. She had left Louisiana years before searching for a better life. After only living in San Francisco for about a year, Pops moved to Compton, California where he stayed with his other grandparents. Here he continued in school and tended to the geese, chickens and string bean field across the street from their home. Soon after, he would move in with his own father in Los Angeles. Wanting to go back to San Francisco to be with his mom, Pops was upset with his dad for sending him back to Louisiana while my grandfather left Los Angeles to follow the auto-industry to Detroit, Michigan. Back in Louisiana, my father re-joined his cousins, who helped him to find a job. As my father worked, he saved up enough money in order to move back to San Francisco to be with his mom.

In Daly City, the next town south of San Francisco, Pops told a story about him and his friends going to the local bowling alley, which they often did on the weekends. He mentioned that on one particular evening the cops came in to harass him and his friends. Gary, Raymond and Michael Jamison, who were all friends of Pops, were there that night. The last call for alcohol was around two in the morning. The cops came in and skipped all the white folks and came straight to Pops and his friends, telling them no alcohol after two. They explained to the cops that they hadn't bought any drinks recently and that the watered-down ones they observed, they were finished with. With threatening demeanors, the officers dumped out the left-over watered-down drinks as part of their intimidating tactics. One of my dad's friends questioned the officers as to why they came straight to them and ignored all the other patrons. They were then asked for their IDs. The cops got aggressive with Jamison as he continued to question why they were being harassed. The cops then got into a tussle with Jamison, who happened to be wearing a pocketless sweatsuit. During the tussle, one of the cops was trying to place a baggie of drugs into Jamison's pocket, not realizing he didn't have any pockets. Once Jamison realized that this police officer was trying to plant drugs on him, he started to holler out that they were trying to frame him! Ultimately, the cops placed Jamison into the police car and took him away.

Pops and his friends decided they would follow these cops back to the police station/jail to ensure their friend was not going to get beaten in some alleyway. As they followed, they noticed the cops were headed in the wrong direction from the jail and police station. The cops soon realized they were being followed by Pops and his friends, so they eventually made their way to the police station. While in custody, Jamison was apparently beaten up by the cops. Jamison, who happened to be a San Francisco police officer, tried explaining himself to these racist Daly City cops, but his explanation meant nothing to them at the time. Needless to say, Jamison was able to later prove that he was a cop, ended up suing Daly City Police and went on to buy himself a brand-new home!

Lighting and Thunder, the name of the softball team that Pops and his friends created, was an awesome sight to see as a young boy. The team was made up of mostly Blacks, one Asian and one Latin brother. What made this team impressionable to me was that there was no team that could beat them. In the league, there would be only a few other teams that were equally talented. The one that was their rival was another all-black team called the Black Orpheus. In some strange way, and as young as I was, it honestly felt good to see Pop's Lighting and Thunder team smack homeruns all day long, destroying any and all teams that they played against. Looking back, having dealt with and been privy to all of the discrimination and oppression tactics imposed on blacks, it gave me a sense of retribution for the unjust treatment. It felt like Black Americans were somewhat equal compared to the inequality and years of subjugation. Finally, on what seemed like an even playing field, Black Americans could not be denied the respect they deserved for once! Even if the referees tried to cheat or wanted to cheat, it was virtually impossible to deny a base hit or a home run. It was actually insane to watch this team beat the shit out of every team they came across. Pops and his team had so many trophies, he hardly had any space to keep them. However, once off the field and the bright field lights turned off, it was back to the reality of living as a Black American in the United States where you knew your "place" in society.

While living in San Francisco, my father recalls being pulled over by the San Francisco police department. He says that the cop told him he had run a stop sign. My father stated he did not run a stop sign and that he had to stop. Not only for the stop sign, but also for a vagrant man crossing the street who had tried to engage my father by rambling off in "jargon" that pops could not understand. As Pops pulled over and parked, my half-brother who was seated in the back-seat of the car, had instinctively pulled off his seatbelt when the car came to a stop. The cop not only cited pops for running the stop sign, but for my half-brother not wearing a seatbelt. So, Pops decided that he would contest the ticket in court. He went to court where he learned that the cop had written up his report to say that he had multiple kids in the car not wearing seatbelts, yet there was only one kid, my half-brother. Pops mentioned that he had never even seen the report. Another NGH racist move by the City's finest!

MY UNCLES

One of my uncles recalls my step-grandfather (fig. 8) as a very hard laborer who had his own tractor and did landscaping in the small southeast Texas town of Port Acres where my mother and her siblings grew up. Because of my step-grandfather's business in the community, he knew a lot of people and knew quite a lot of white folks. One day, as my uncle was working alongside his step-father, one of his white friends stopped by for small talk. Admiring the work that my uncle was doing, the man asked my step-grandfather if he would mind lending my uncle to him to help him work on a big boat that he was building. He offered to pay my uncle. My step-grandfather asked my uncle if he would like to go work for the guy and my uncle eagerly accepted the offer. As my uncle found himself at this white man's home, he was fond of the beauty of the man's property and the enormous size of this boat that they were building. There were lots of people working on the boat, including the man's sons, brother and a friend. As my uncle began to work, the man was impressed by his work skills. The man asked my uncle if he had any friends that would be interested in helping as well. My uncle said that his close friend may be interested, so the man drove back to my uncle's neighborhood about six miles away where they found his friend. His friend also accepted the offer. As they all worked, lunchtime came. The white man's wife had prepared lunch for all of them. They were called to wash up and come have lunch, so my uncle said as he finished washing up and made his way into the house and to the dining table. Before he could sit down, the wife came in the dining area and saw my uncle getting ready to take a place at the table. She immediately yelled out to her husband, and he came running in. He escorted my uncle back to the yard. He told him that he and his friend could not eat with them in the house and at their table and he then showed my uncle and his friend a couple of upside-down barrels in the yard where their lunch was served. However, my uncle, obviously and righteously upset, told his friend that he was not going to eat. When questioned as to why by his friend, my uncle responded that he didn't want to work for these people any longer. He felt unworthy, un-important and used. He told his friend, "let's go", but his friend was hungry. Despite the humiliation, his friend wanted to earn money. My uncle ended up walking the six miles back home alone. Although this incident took place not more than 20 years prior to my first encounter with NGH, the experience that my uncle felt was just that, NGH!

Figure 8 Early 70's, Step-grandfather, at the family farm

My other uncle stated, "Color blind to white and black-skinned parents" is how he recalls growing up as a Black American. My grandmother, my uncle's mother, was a very fair and very light- skinned woman. In hindsight, my grand-mother was a "white" woman! I never thought or contem-plated her racial background. I always saw her as just being my grandmother! Her jet-black hair was long and wavy. However, my mother would later tell me after I became more aware of color and race, that "you best not refer to your grandmother as a white person, she would be very offended!".. As for my uncle's statement regarding being color blind, so was I. I never saw my grandmother as white or black. I never saw my German aunt, who is married to my uncle, as a white woman. I never thought anything strange of my great uncle and his Asian wife. This was my normal! I was color blind until this nasty society full of racists, bigots and white supremacists tarnished my innocence. My uncle recalls segregation in his small childhood town in Louisiana. My mother and father would reflect from time to time, so did my uncle as he recalled the water fountains and restrooms labeled as colored and whites only. My uncle states that in addition to segregated municipalities, so were the parks. He adds that he didn't realize he was living in a segregated small town until he became more aware as a teenager and then living in Texas. Obviously, being bi-racial, my uncle's appearance resembles more black features than white. He stated that the town he grew up in as a kid was segregated into three parts. The whites lived on the other side of the railroad tracks, the blacks lived on the opposite side of town and the majority of mixed families lived in between.

The discussion about skin color or race on either side of the family, as my uncle would explain, never came up. "There was little playtime for us. Being young, it was a way of life there and you never had time to concentrate on race," is what my uncle explained. My uncle went on to talk about his grandparents and how one set of grandparents were white, and his other set of grandparents were black. He also mentioned his oldest brother, who lived his entire life in Louisiana, often got into fights with white men over racism. My uncle enlisted in the United States Army in the mid-1950s and was stationed in Germany. He met my aunt, a German woman. They fell in love, and he attempted to marry her. The clergy on base in Germany stated that my uncle could not marry my auntie because a black man marrying a white woman had to be rich. Determined to solidify their love, my uncle and auntie snuck into a German church in the city of Bamberg where they "unofficially" exchanged their vows. Later, my uncle enlisted his uncles who were back in San Francisco for help to sponsor my aunt in order to get her to the states, which proved successful. Once back in the States, they would soon be officially married. While visiting his hometown in Texas, my uncle had two very close friends that he grew up with and one of those friends did not like the fact that my uncle married a white woman. He decided not to associate with him any longer.

My step-grandfather, as I mentioned, owned his own landscaping business and knew lots of people around town. He owned his own tractor and raised farm animals. He had a very strong work ethic and passed that down to my uncles. During his end of life (I happened to be around 16 years of age) and while visiting with my grandmother in Texas, I was there the day my step-grandfather passed away. I had been visiting with my grandmother for about two weeks prior and it was time for me to head back home to California. As funeral arrangements were being made, my family from California were making arrangements to fly into Texas for the funeral service. I had to get back home to go to work, but I was glad I was there for my grandmother during the passing of her husband.

Years later, my grandmother had moved in with my mother and step-father. My mom was taking care of her during her last years of life. My grandmother passed away in 2006 and we had services for her in California, then later in Texas where she would be laid to rest next to her husband. I had learned that despite my grandmother and step-grandfather being poor, they were able to secure plots in the cemetery. My step-grandfather would often work at the cemetery helping to dig holes with his tractor. The owners of the cemetery paid him by offering him two burial sites. Once my grandmother's body was taken back to Texas to her hometown and it was time to head to the cemetery, it was amazing to see the respect that the local Black community had for her. We drove past citizens who stopped in their tracks to pay tribute as we passed by in the funeral procession. I had never seen anything like this back in California! I noticed that the majority of the people on the streets paid their respects as we continued towards the cemetery, and in that moment, it felt like human beings cared and that your life meant something even to those that did not know you.

As we embarked on the cemetery grounds, I noticed that the entrance to the cemetery was well manicured. The headstones and tombs appeared organized in rows, clean and orderly. As we made our way through the front part of the cemetery, we started to make our way into an area that wasn't so orderly looking and nicely manicured. I began to think, *what is up with the contrast?* I inquired about the difference. I learned that it was custom, and maybe even law, that Black Americans were to be buried in the back of the cemetery. White Americans were buried in the front. Well, damn, wouldn't you know, even in death you are segregated!

MY GRANDFATHER

Born in Branch, Louisiana September 21, 1921, my Grandfather Antoine Melancon had a simple but funny story to share that stands out as clear as day in his mind when I interviewed him on November 12, 2020. He is 99-years of age and of sound mind. He knows and recalls all of his family by name down to his great grandchildren! He gets up early in the morning every day for exercise which includes push-ups and stairs. Living upstairs in a two-story home with my father and step-mother, he makes several daily trips up and down from his bedroom to the kitchen where he still cooks his own food! My Grandfather recalls working in the sugar cane, rice, wheat and cotton fields, as well as cutting wood. He recalls liking to work in the sugar cane fields but hated to pick cotton. He remembers the days that blacks were not allowed in the restaurants, and if there was a restaurant that allowed blacks, they would have to enter through the back door. He stated that he was a very good swimmer and would often swim in the rivers and bayous in Crowley, Louisiana where he grew up. When asked how he learned how to swim, he stated his cousins threw him in the water. He stated that was the way blacks learned how to swim in those days. You know that saying you either "sink or swim"? Luckily for him and my father, this self-taught way to learn to swim actually worked for them. However, for many other blacks that did not work and many subsequently lost their lives to drowning. My grandfather stated that he was such a good swimmer, the community would often ask him to search the canals and bayous for the bodies of the unlucky and unfortunate blacks who drowned. He stated that only one time he was able to recover a body. I asked him about the dangers of animals such as alligators when swimming in these waters. Although there are lots of alligators in the waters throughout Louisiana, he stated that where he was, there weren't any. He did say that there were plenty of snakes. He stated that in the water, the snake could not bite you because when they opened up their mouths it would fill with water making it impossible to bite you.

I asked my grandfather if he had any recollection of his grandfather, to which he replied yes. He went on to explain that his grandfather was able to acquire hundreds of acres of land back in the late 1800s. The land would be left to his family, but because the surviving family had poor reading skills, white authority had them sign documents that they thought would solidify their ownership only to realize they signed over their rights of the lands to the white folks, wrongly thinking they were securing the property for themselves. This practice was quite common during those days regarding ex-slaves who were able to obtain and own property, where whites would "legally" steal lands from them.

My grandfather talked about the days of going to the movies as a teenager with his friends in town. Blacks were allowed to go to the same movie theaters with whites, but they were made to sit separately. In those days' movie theaters had balconies, which is where the blacks had to sit while the whites took seats on the first level. When the bottom level seats were all occupied, whites would take to the balcony and the blacks had to move to the rear. My grandfather stated that if the whites ran out of seats the blacks were forced out of the theater all together, even if they paid. Of course, they did not get a refund. Whenever the black teenagers were able to get in, at the end of the movies when coming down the stair-well, the white kids would be waiting for them, ready to taunt and physically assault them. But this never kept my grandfather and his friends from going. One day they came up with a plan of how to deal with the situation the next time they went to the movies. Rather than come all the way down the stairs, they would stop mid-way and leap over the stair-rail and would land on top of the awaiting white kids. Once on top of them they would get into a brief fight, often beating them up, and they would run as fast as they could to get away. He said they were never caught as they would easily out-run them.

MY GREAT, GREAT GRANDFATHER

At the age of 17, Thomas Simon Sr., my great, great grandfather, arrived in Iberia Perish, Freetown, Louisiana, from Virginia, where he settled down and had 11 children. During his lifetime in Freetown, he had acquired 500 acres of land, which was recorded in 1882. He had divided these acres amongst his children. The family worked their fields and crops daily, and when the weather was bad and/or rainy, the men would gather in front of their store across the street from a preacher's house and would spend the day talking. On one stormy and rainy day, August 16, 1888, there would be a riot known as the Iberia Riot. Commonly known to family members as the Simon Massacre. During the course of the week, twenty white vigilantes had made their way into Freetown due to a growing concern of a revenge plot being orchestrated by black citizens from the town. It was reported to the whites earlier that there were somewhere between five to six hundred blacks in Freetown who were arming themselves with Winchester rifles, old muskets and double-barreled shotguns. By mid-week, it was further reported that the numbers of armed blacks had doubled and were steadily increasing. "The citizens rode into Freetown and found, as rumored, a large number of armed negroes quartered there. They asked its meaning, and the negroes were silent. They then demanded a surrender of their arms, with the promise that when they learned to behave themselves, they would be returned, and that the negroes should at once disperse. The great majority of them accepted the terms of the party and surrendered their arms, which were found without exception to be loaded with ball or buckshot" (The New Orleans, 1888). As most of the armed blacks laid down their weapons, there were at least twenty remaining blacks who refused to surrender. By this time, more whites on horses showed up in the numbers of about 150 to 200, at which point the blacks took refuge in the preacher's house. Soon after, a white messenger came to the house and informed the blacks that they had 20 minutes to comply and surrender their guns. Prior to the 20-minute deadline, a shot rang out, a horse was injured and a shootout ensued that lasted for about an hour and a half. Four to five hundred shots were exchanged, leaving my great, great grandfather dead along with his son, two sons-in-laws and several other blacks from the community.

The whole story behind the massacre was that my great, great grandfather's two sons and his son-in-law by the name of Andy Smith, were being accused by white folks for apparently "stealing" cattle, cotton and corn from the outlying white communities. "Several of these negroes are reported to have been whipped for it, but it was not possible to detect the ringleader, Andy Smith". Learning that the whites were going to whip him, Smith apparently sent word back to the white folks that he and his friends would be ready for them. Smith was then accused of retaliation, due to informing his community of his situation, as they secured weapons for protection. Due to this bold and courageous move by the twenty blacks that remained steadfast, the surrounding nearby towns of white citizens were feeling a bit uneasy about possible retaliation.

"There is great uneasiness among the negroes who fear repetition of violent acts in this quarter. Many of the whites are supplying themselves with arms and ammunition in case of need while it is rumored that there is a move to organize a guard for the protection of the town. It is safe to say, however, that no bloodshed need be feared at this place, so the sober judgment of our citizens may be relied on to tide over the present uneasy state of affairs". Another historical periodical, most likely authored by a white publisher, reported the following: "The war against the disorderly characters is not ended by the slaughter at Freetown. The white people are generally opposed to acts of violence, except where armed opposition is looked for. The people of Broussardville have organized 100 men for protection, and the hundred at Scott's are all armed with Winchesters. Yet both companies declare they will not inaugurate violence, only protect their homes from reprisal and spoliation. They are organized into an oath-bound league all over the State. And cases have occurred already where white men have been assassinated by mysterious men after disobeying repeated warnings" (The New York Times, 1888). If you take note of this article, you will see how easily media reports can manipulate and be propagandized. Were my ancestors wrong for wanting to avoid being brutalized by white folks in power, based on accusations and rumors? To report that they were an "armed opposition" is exactly how it is spun in these current times. They were looking to protect themselves from the threat of being whipped, or worse yet, lynched. But as the article would suggest, being black and armed calls for the slaughter of people and that they had it coming! Ultimately the 500 acres that my great, great grandfather obtained was now seized and in the hands of whites. This would not be the only massacre during these early days but part of a trend of massacres committed against Black Americans.

OTHER HISTORICAL MASSACRES

Prior to the Simon Massacre, in September 1868, approximately 250 Black Americans would be slaughtered for political reasons in what was known as the Opelousas Massacre, which took place in St. Landry Parish, Louisiana. During those days, Black Americans were able to vote for a short period in time, and because Republicans were winning both state and local elections due to the huge number of Black American voters ranging in the thousands, Democratic whites were not happy. The reader needs to understand that 1800s Republicans and Democrats were not the same as modern day Republicans and Democrats. Don't let the current, modern-day political agenda convince you that republicans are for Black equal rights the way they were in historical times. The early day Republicans were helping newly freed slaves gain their independence and Democrats were typically confederate racists who did not want change. Again, it is very important to note that those early day Republicans are not the Republicans of today, and the

Democrats of today are very different from the Democrats of the past. A Republican teacher and editor from Ohio went to Opelousas to help newly freed slaves become independent and politically involved. He was met with opposition by white Democrats, and in response, white supremacist groups were formed and thousands of white men formed lynch mobs. The Ohio teacher/editor was reported to have been taken or even killed, and in response, a group of Black Americans was preparing for his rescue. This would be rumored amongst the whites that the blacks were planning a rebellion and were increasingly gaining arms, and since the November presidential election was on the horizon, voter suppression and fear by the Democratic whites would fuel the soon to come massacre. From that point on, white supremacist groups in the thousands would set out to intimidate and kill hundreds of Black Americans that included women and children and even some sympathetic whites. The massacre lasted for about two weeks. "The Opelousas massacre also set the stage for future acts of violence and intimidation. Lynching became routinized in Louisiana, a systematic way by which whites sought to assert white supremacy in response to African- American resistance" (Boissoneault, 2018).

In 1873, the Colfax Massacre took place, also in Louisiana, which played a huge part in giving rise to Jim Crow laws and segregation. Whites wanted to continue their way of life prior to the Civil War, which included owning slaves. "During that time, thousands of African-Americans were killed by domestic terrorists like the Ku Klux Klan, who tried to reinforce antebellum policies of white supremacy. Immediately after the end of the Civil War, different factions began fighting over power. Bitter over the Confederacy's loss, many white Southern Democrats tried their best to continue disenfranchising and restricting the rights of former slaves" (Boissoneault, the 1873 Colfax Massacre Crippled the Reconstruction Era, 2018). Because of the recent Governor's election, it was a highly contested split between Republican and Democrat, and seemingly, the Republican seat had been won. After fearing that white Democrats would attempt to take control over the local parish, a group of black militias would take guard and occupy the courthouse. Consequently, white Democrats, many made up of former slave owners, formed armed groups such as the "White League". A group of over 100 white militia showed up in force and surrounded the courthouse. They fired a cannon into the courthouse and a shootout ensued. Outgunned and outnumbered, many blacks were killed, and the rest had surrendered. Those that surrendered were either shot or hung. A total of about 150 Black Americans were killed during the battle, whereas only three whites were killed.

Later in 1921, the Black Wall Street Massacre took place in Tulsa, Oklahoma, the wealthiest place in America for blacks at the time. The massacre was carried out by an angry white mob, where approximately 26 Black Americans were killed. Homes and businesses were targeted. This massacre was sparked after a teenage black boy was "accused of assaulting" a teenage white girl.

These moments in history shine a light into today's conflict with white supremacy, racism and hatred towards Black Americans, which equates to the birth of fear. The fear of uprisings and retaliation by blacks was real during slavery and, more importantly, soon after the abolishment of slavery in 1865. Whites must have been in fear due to the thousands and thousands of Africans they brought over to the States, so many to the point where the numbers of blacks were just about equal or were outnumbering the white population. "In the middle of the eighteenth century, perhaps 200,000 white persons in the continental colonies lived in neighborhoods where Negroes outnumbered them. And the population of the colonies, which later became the United States, taken as a whole contained a higher proportion of Negroes in the period 1730-1765 than at any other time in the nation's history. In many of the areas, one of the major daily concerns of responsible men was the effective control of masses of slaves" (Jordan, 1968). The bondage, brutality, atrocities, torture, rapes, murders and countless acts of horrendous treatment perpetuated by white slave owners for hundreds of years, and then all of a sudden, the Emancipation Proclamation!

Ahh shit, greediness has gotten the ex-slave owners in a predicament, or a "pickle" like white folks would say. Set free after over 200 years and the population of Black Americans is huge! Yeah, a sense of fear should be warranted, as retaliation is a must for many, and it is what makes many of us human! Whether it is right or wrong, it is a natural fact. In my opinion however, this fear was unfounded by whites. Blacks did not have the weaponry or gun power equal to the numbers that whites did. How could they? I am sure that most recently-freed blacks at the time were more concerned about their survival rather than retribution. With lack of resources, I am sure most freed slaves were only concerned with their living arrangements, how they would sustain their lives or perhaps finding and reuniting with family members that had been torn away and lost through the slave trade. Nevertheless, white leaders would instill fear amongst other whites and you begin to see this common thread in the examples of these massacres.

"St. Landrails reacted to armed Negroes and rumors of an uprising in the same manner that Southerners had reacted for generations" (Biozonal, The Deadliest Massacre in Reconstruction-Era Louisiana Happened 150 Years Ago, 2018). Armed Black Americans! I am sure many were armed, but again, I am sure many, many more whites were armed and had unlimited stockpiles of ammo. How do you think they were able to pull off slavery in the first place!?

The force and power of the gun! I am pretty sure it wasn't through the force of hand-to-hand combat! Whites have always had the upper hand with this form of weaponry. But they want folks to believe that a stolen people, far away and generations from their homeland, had the resources to have access to guns. As if Black Americans were gun suppliers. However, convincingly enough, over and over, the fear persisted. Consequently, this fear would be forever sealed in the hearts and minds of whites and blacks for generations to come that still exists today. This fear of the past perpetuated by false literature, manipulation, propaganda and stereotypes into the future, has given way to the discrimination, prejudice, bigotry, racism and hate that we continue to see today. This has proven consequential for the well-being of Black America and America as a whole, as exemplified in modern-day uprisings, lootings, riots, property destruction and even loss of life. My experiences, extremely minor in comparison to those of my ancestors and the countless killings of Black American men and boys today, is proof that racism, as well as systemic racism, has been part of the American fabric ever since colonization.

OTHER MASSACRES
THAT SHOULD BE NOTED

New Orleans, Louisiana-New Orleans Massacre, July 1866. 50 Black Americans were killed due to disputes in social structure and the continuation of the Civil War.

St. Bernard Parish, Louisiana-St. Bernard Massacre, 1868. 135 Black Americans were killed due to political voter suppression.

The Thibodaux, Louisiana-Thibodaux Massacre, November 1887. 35 Black Americans were killed due to Labor disputes.

Many more massacres and uprisings plagued America, and like the butcher who worked at Safeway in my hometown who hated the Vietnamese as a Vietnamese war veteran, his hate would continue long after the war. Who knows, maybe his views of hate would spread and continue with his offspring, his grandchildren and great-grandchildren. Just as with the Civil War and freed Black Americans who fought for their freedom, hate would prevail amongst the confederates at a huge cost to Black Americans for generations to come. Hate is taught not born, and when an innocent little girl can say to the face of a Black American, "Look, grandma, it's a nigger," we clearly understand that hate is alive and thriving.

These massacres were carried out behind fear, fear that Democratic confederates were losing power just as they had lost the Civil War and who wanted to continue with their ways of life prior to the war. From employment to voting rights, housing and segregation, the confederate ideology represented, and continues to represent, pure hate, evil and a liking to terrorize Black Americans. That is what the confederate flag represents. Seeing these confederate flags flying in the back of pickup trucks is highly unsettling. It sends a strong racist message and reminds me of all the Black Americans who lost their lives at the hands of racist people. I think of poor Mr. James Byrd of Texas. If you forgot, or have not heard about the story of Mr. Byrd, he was a black man who was offered a ride in 1998 by a white guy he had known most of his life. The man had several friends with him who were all white supremacists. They took Mr. Byrd to a field and beat him. They then tied his ankles with chains and attached these chains to the back of their pickup truck and drug him along an asphalt road for about three miles until he was dismembered. They got out of the truck to gather Mr. Byrd's body parts and took his body parts to be dumped in front of a Black Church. A pure act of evil!

Tribute goes out to all the innocent African/Black Americans whose lives were lost in a new world whose only wish was to live free. They didn't ask to be here, they didn't want to be here, they didn't want to lose their families, languages, cultures and their ways of life. They were brought here by force, forced to be used for hard labor, only considered as property, not human. They were then consumed and discarded like a huge plate of left-over food! They have been blamed for this and accused of that, threatened for wanting equality, threatened for wanting to live! They were murdered by the thousands in a quest for extinction, but here we are collectively as a people. Black Americans are still here, still alive and most importantly, still wanting to live free, free of discrimination, free of harassment and yearning for a racist-free America!

WHY DO THEY HATE US SO MUCH?

This book was not written as a research project but as a personal account, drawing on the experiences of my own life with a few stories from those that are close to me. Without researching why they hate us so much, I will attempt to answer this question based on what I have learned throughout the years. These are only my expressed opinions.

Skin color. It was reported that in the mid-1500's, the English, long before they ever came across a black person, already had their perceptions on what the color black meant to them. However, and in contrast, the Spanish viewed their first encounter with a black person with a bit of appreciation and respect towards this difference in other humans.

"A Spanish chronicle translated into English in 1555 was filled with wonder at this diversity: "one of the marvelous thynges that god useth in the composition of man, is coloure: which doubtless can not be considered without great admiration in beholding one to be white and another blacke, beige colored utterly contrary, sum likewise to be yellow which is between blacke and white: and other of other colours as it were of dyvers liveres." As this passage suggests, the juxtaposition of black and white was the most striking marvel of all. And for Englishmen this juxtaposition was more than a curiosity.

Long before they found that some men were black, Englishmen found in the idea of blackness a way of expressing some of their most ingrained values. No other color except white conveyed so much emotional impact. As described in the *Oxford English Dictionary*, the meaning of *black* before the sixteenth century included, "Deeply stained with dirt; soiled, dirty, foul...Having dark or deadly purposes, malignant; pertaining to or involving death, heady; baneful, disastrous, sinister...Foul, iniquitous, atrocious, horrible wicked... Indicating disgrace, censure, liability to punishment, etc". Black was an emotionally partisan color, the handmaid and symbol of baseness and evil, a sign of danger and repulsion. Embedded in the concept of blackness was its direct opposite-whiteness. No other colors so clearly implied opposition, "beige colors utterly contrary". No other was so frequently used to denote polarization: "Every white will have its blacke, And every sweet it's sowre". White and black connotated purity and filthiness, virginity and sin, virtue and baseness, beauty and ugliness, beneficence and evil, God and the devil" (Jordan, 1968).

The English, who understood the color black as noted in their dictionary in the 1500s, meant all things with negative descriptions such as bad, ugly and evil and to refer to their first encounters with these people of color from Africa as black. Therefore, it's easy to conclude that perhaps this meaning would affect generation after generation and how, until this very day, these views are still held regarding Black Americans. Because of their Oxford dictionary meaning of the word black; Is this why they hate us so much?

NGH. What does that mean to me? What does that mean to you? What does that mean to the folks who take the time to write the phrase, say the phrase, who think blacks should go "home"? As a kid, when I first observed NGH, I did not realize it was in reference to me and others who look like me, and I soon learned once I was called a NIGGER by white folks, this realization. NGH did not mean for me to go to my current residence, did not mean to go live with my father and did not mean move to my mom and dad's hometown in the south. I used to think that it meant for me and all other blacks in America to go to Africa. But I would often contemplate that. How would that look? How would that take place? How would we know where to go in Africa? The Black American is centuries away from his original roots, with no customs and no names. How would we be identified? Would we find long lost cousins? Hell, as you really think about what that looks like, it begins to sound more and more ridiculous, 400 years later! History tells us our ancestors were brought here to America as slaves. They were made to lose their identities, forced to drop their African names and to take on the names their slave masters gave them.

They were split and broken up as families and were sold away to never be seen again by one another. Customs were lost and the African in America, generation after generation, became less "African". As a result, the Black American was born at no fault of his or her own and is consequently here in America with no ties or families or landmarks in Africa. America is the birth home for Black Americans, thanks to greedy passions of early European settlers. The "forefathers" are responsible for the birth of blacks in America, so if some of you folks are mad because we are here, don't be mad at us. Be mad at those depicted in historic pictures on the walls of your homes and businesses. We had no control over our destiny to end up in America. As much as some would like us to go back to Africa, we are here to stay as the African Ancestors, as well as the European Ancestors who have been here since the beginning and at the same time. Black people here in America are Americans, just like white folks. NGH to me means that whoever chants the phrase or writes that phrase is a racist and whoever refers to the Black American as a NIGGER is a racist. It seems to me that things could be a bit easier for the racists now left in this country to go elsewhere and try to discover new lands or planets to inhabit. Since the world is pretty much occupied, maybe once they find a new habitable planet, they can colonize there. But this time, don't be so lazy. Don't bring with you any Asians, Mexicans or Blacks to do the hard labor for you. The rest of us can stay here and repair planet Earth from all the racist damage that has been done by people who hate people. Home for the Black American is here in America. Despite all the hate and racism, Black Americans as a whole have been kind, loving people, willing to lend a hand to anyone. Is this why they hate us so much? Is it because we won't leave America and we won't disappear from America?

As a Bachelor of Social Work graduate from the California State University, Sacramento, and after earning an Associate of Arts Degree attending community colleges, I have had the opportunity to enroll in various courses regarding American History, and more specifically, ones with a Black American focus. From the late 1500s, when the first 20 African indentured servants made landfall, through the slave trade, abolishment of slavery in the late 1800s, Jim Crow and the civil rights movement and up until the present, I have gained a wealth of information. From propaganda slogans to current day media attacks, Black Americans have been the target of dehumanizing ads to paint a picture to the rest of the world that instills fear in those who have limited to no contact with Black Americans. During the slave trade era, slaves were treated worse than some animals on their way to the slaughterhouse. Africans were beaten, tortured and killed if they did not submit to the control of the slave holders. Torture included whippings with whips that left lifelong scars, to killings that included shootings, hangings, drownings, burnings, etc. If any living thing on this earth was exposed or is exposed to this form of abuse and atrocity and terror, then the one who is subjecting the group to this form of treatment must know that the treatment is cruel and inhumane. Slave owners were totally aware that they were playing with fire, due to the treatment they subjected their African slaves to. There must have been a sense of fear, perhaps mild, by the European colonizers due to the availability of resources, logistics, materials and weaponry at the ready. For the African slave, there was no availability to resources, the lands were foreign, and they had nothing but the skin on their backs. They had no possession or control of weapons to match that of their slave owners. Consequently, the African slave had to submit or die. The consciousness of these slave owners must have been filled with paranoia, knowing that the pain they inflicted on the helpless slaves and the suffering they caused could result in serious backlash. There were few uprisings amongst slaves who were able to get their hands on some form of weaponry and seriously injure or kill their slave owners and their families. These uprisings proved that slaves were not in servitude willingly and were totally aware of the inhumane treatment that was subjected upon them. If freed, whites feared ex-slaves would come back at them seeking revenge and justice in retaliation for the harsh treatment they endured for a couple hundred years. This fear is a direct result of current day racism. Is this fear part of the reason why they hate us so much?

Images of Black Americans soon after they were emancipated were depicted as savages and bloodthirsty heathens on a mission to rape and kill White Americans. As the fake news spread throughout the south, numerous white lynch mobs were formed in a hunt for blacks and widespread lynching for decades to follow. As mentioned previously, Black Americans had very little resources in this foreign land once they were freed. The economic way of life was established and achieved by whites through slave labor. At first, some Black Americans were allowed to own property, which one could imagine was necessary to create stability and a foundation for the basic human rights needed for survival. Unfortunately, at that time, blacks had to rely on whites in order to make their new way of life, living in a new "free" America. Initially, blacks would be promised land in which to grow their own crops, as in the example of both of my great, great grandfathers who were able to acquire lots of land. However, this would soon be stopped by whites through the fear of Black Americans gaining more power. So, the propaganda ensued and resulted in this country's fate full of hate. The hate has been so ingrained into the unconscious soul of the modern-day racists. Is this why the scrolled words NIGGERS GO HOME was so prevalent as I grew up as a young child? Is the unconscious racist one whose thought process is based on primitive thinking, unable to perform or understand the complexities of human genealogy or to understand simple human rights? Is this why they hate us so much?

I wondered as a boy, *why do these white people hate me so much? Why do they scream out NIGGER with rage in their eyes and evil in their voices? Why? What did I do?* I realized it was not what I did or what my ancestors did. It was what their ancestors did and the hate rhetoric that was passed down from generation to generation. I bet these modern-day racist people don't even know where their hate comes from, like in the example of that little girl in Safeway who casually stated, "Look grandma, it's a NIGGER". That was over 30 years ago. I wonder how that little girl turned out. Did she eventually reject that racist hate that her family instilled in her or realize that racist ideology is one of the lowest demonizing forms of the human soul ? Did she abandon and ultimately reject it through the grace of God in search of enlightenment? Racism and hate are taught and have been taught since slaves were brought to America, out of fear of retaliation and uprising by Black America. Out of that, perhaps they feared that the Black American would someday hold equal value and rights along with them. They believed that blacks were more or less animals rather than human beings. In today's times, stereotypes help to keep the racist fire lit, and carried out not only by whites, but also by other non-whites. For example, my closest friend in high school was dating a Mexican girl. She would tell him that if her father were ever to find out she was dating a black guy, that he would disown her. Some of my other ethnic friends have stated that their parents told them, "If you date anyone outside of our ethnicity, just make sure the person is not black". Why do these non-white minorities feel this way? Are they just as racist as white racist people? Perhaps what they see in the media played a major role in their attitudes and perceptions of Black Americans. Is this why they hate us so much?

Awareness, education and an open and sound mind without prejudice is what people need in order to see others as individuals and not collectively as a group. The behavior of some does not equal the behavior of all for any particular group of people. How simple, small-minded and ignorant for America to fall for those stereotypes which are upheld by the media. For example, the media typically portrays women holding a certain image and body type, and because of that, people fall for it, and it becomes a major issue for those seeking to look like what the media portrays. People subject themselves to harmful medical procedures such as plastic surgeries without understanding or being aware of the consequences. If you haven't seen the TV show Botched, check it out and you will know what I am talking about. All sorts of insecure folks seek to enhance their appearances when there was nothing wrong with their appearances in the first place. The same works for media images of Black Americans. The day-time TV talk and drama shows, along with the evening news, overwhelmingly depict Black Americans as criminals and dysfunctional. Sitcom shows of the 1970s like Good Times feature a Black American family living in the projects. The theme song suggests that these are in fact "good times" for Black Americans, as they live in poverty and crowded run-down conditions. What these shows are saying to its viewers is that all blacks are criminals, they all live-in poverty and that Black Americans are content with that way of living. The majority of my black friends and family members do not live that way. Many are successful, many have money, and some may be considered as living upscale lives. But no matter how much money you have and how successful you are, when the Black American walks into the auto dealership, the department store, the real estate office and the medical office, we are often seen as not belonging there, intent to steal or intended to waste people's time. You have to blame American media and racist politicians for upholding these overwhelming perceptions and stereotypes. Is this why they hate us so much?

A therapist and friend to my mother, a Jewish guy, had built up the courage one day to share a story with her. Short and stocky in stature, he had explained that as an adolescent athlete he had a fixation with the physical appearance of other black athletes. He stated that he was concerned about competitive athletics and how his body and abilities would stand up and be competitive against the black athletes. He and his other white friends paid much attention to their own muscle development and often compared themselves to one another. However, when comparing themselves to the black athletes, they felt that they had much better muscle definition than themselves and were often envious. Does this envy produce hate for some and for another, possibility or reason for why they hate us so much?

Athletic, muscular and tall, all the characteristics that he wished he carried, Snyder characterized the black athlete as superior "because of his high thighs that go up into his back". He sourced this opinion in antebellum times, "when during the slave trading, the slave owner would breed his big black to his big woman so that he would have a big black kid". Snyder, also known as "Jimmy the Greek" Snyder, a sports prognosticator, also went on to say years ago, that "They've (blacks) got everything," he said. "If they take over coaching like everybody wants them to, there's not going to be anything left for white people" (Lawrence, 2018). Snyder later regretted these statements. However, one must question his thinking behind the comment. Was Jimmy the Greek Snyder feeling somewhat like my mother's Jewish friend, envious and perhaps jealous? But rather than expressing the desire or wishing to be more like the physical appearance of a black athlete, Snyder expressed his issue out of fear, fear of whites losing coaching and sports reporting jobs to blacks. Taking a look at both scenarios, you realize that they have the potential to produce the same outcome of emotion for those that are envious and jealous: the emotion of hate. Is this why they hate us so much?

"To be honest, I think that inherent fear comes from our history. For whatever reason, we as black men are looked at as the ones who are going to harm your daughters, the ones who are most likely to rob and steal and kill. Historically, dating back all the way to slavery, the picture that's been painted of black males- you're not educated enough, you're just a breaker, a mule- continues to permeate our psyche and culture" (Wright, 2016). Is this why they hate us so much?

I wonder if those that hate Black Americans understand the history of how Black Americans arrived in this country and what it took for them to survive. I wonder if those whites that hate us understand that blacks in America are a result of their ancestors luring, capturing and taking Africans from their homelands across the Atlantic to a land inhabited by indigenous peoples (then killing off the indigenous peoples in order to settle and colonize America on the backs of enslaved blacks). I wonder if those that hate us understand that our ancestors here in America, the ones who were freed in the late 1800s, had nothing. I wonder if the ones that hate us understand that without a foundation, without a culture, without access to the necessary resources for survival in a foreign land, how daunting the task would be for any group of people in their struggle for survival. I wonder if those that hate us understand that hating us led to our oppression, suppression and in a cultural perspective, regression in the sense that Black Americans would now be born again. Once freed from slavery, and after hundreds of years of bondage, there would be no going back to Africa. Freed Black Americans in a foreign land with virtually no possessions, suddenly thrusted in a system which quickly and systematically excluded them, had to rely on the "new" White America as they established and held land and property laws. Where would the freed blacks live and how would they survive? Did those that hate us understand that all ancestral and family ties were cut the moment slaves arrived in America? Did those that hate us, that wanted to see us go back to Africa, understand that there was no means to go back to Africa? Did those that hate us understand that the laws they created would do more harm to Black Americans than good? Do those that hate us realize the Black American's livelihood would rest on the shoulders of their ancestors for survival? The response that I imagine would come from the simple-minded confederate racist is that they could care less and would rather see us all eliminated. Because there are remnants of the confederacy ideology still being played out amongst politics, politicians, the media, racist white citizens and white supremacists, this is the reason why organizations like BLM are birthed—because folks in power in America let us know every day that our lives are not important enough to matter and allows American born terrorists to continue with their baseless agendas, harassing, torturing and killing of Black Americans.

POLITICAL REFLECTIONS AND CURRENT HAPPENINGS

William Barr, the United States Attorney General, in June of 2020, stated that he did not believe there's systemic racism among white policing, along with other top officials who, I must add, were older white men. I always find it odd that people who do not experience systemic racism often say there isn't systemic racism, which makes me question whether or not they are racists. But what is even more disturbing is there are Black Americans who honestly think racism doesn't exist, including some very notable and successful celebrities. I am ashamed to know that a couple of them are celebrities that I happen to like and have supported them by buying their products. There are plenty of white folks, men and women, who acknowledge and understand that systemic racism is a real thing. I would like to thank those for believing and seeing racism for what it is and has been for hundreds of years here in America. Many of these white men and women have supported blacks in the battles for equality, and for them and many others who support the equality of black lives and all lives, black men such as myself appreciate and have much respect for others willing to join and support movements seeking remedies to end the virus of racism afflicted upon all minorities.

"Make America Great Again" is the slogan used by Donald Trump, who held a rally in Oklahoma on June 20, 2020. Ninety-nine years earlier, the Black Wall Street Massacre took place, not far from where the rally was being held. This rally was being held during the middle of the worldwide COVID-19 pandemic. Health leaders had been warning about holding gatherings, practicing social distancing and wearing masks, all of which have been ignored by Trump himself and the thousands of his followers. The large crowd of Trump's supporters' waved signs in the air that said "Make America Great Again" while wearing MAGA hats. Are these hats symbolic of the Klansman's infamous hoods? If not, it would seem like it. Make America Great for who? The first time I heard that bullshit slogan, all I could think about was slavery and racism and the continued struggle for equal rights for Black Americans. Insensitive as fuck!

I guess the "Make America Great Again" slogan is meant for one type of people with the confederate mindset and evil intention. How does making America Great Again look to these folks? I bet they would love to have their slaves back. I am sure that would be on their list of making American

Great Again. I am sure if they could send all Mexicans to Mexico, that would be on their list to "Make America Great Again". As long as they can maintain wealth and build wealth on the backs of minorities, ensuring minorities stay beneath them. And who are those black folks attending Trump rallies holding up those same signs? Herman Cain, a huge Trump supporter and prior Presidential candidate, was in attendance. Since Trump viewed mask-wearing as some sort of weakness, almost all of his supporters would be mask-less at this convention. Needless to say, it is August 21, 2020, and during this time period Herman Cain has unfortunately passed away from the virus. Did he contract this virus at the mask-less Trump rally? Who knows, but it doesn't seem like Trump could give a shit! Hell, did he even acknowledge or give respect to this successful "African" American man whose idol seemed to be Trump? Did his life matter to the Republican party? You barely heard a word of the unfortunate event of this man's passing. The nation recognized the George Floyd service and the real civil rights leader John Lewis' service. Seems like America as a whole is ready for a non-racist country by this display. And as far as the confederate ideology goes? Oh well, you tried massacres in the past, you continually oppress and kill Black Americans, but it hasn't worked out in the past. It's not working out in the present and it will surely not work in the future with all this diversity nowadays in America.

Racist people are now a minority in America when it comes to the numbers of Latin Americans, Asian Americans, non-racist White Americans, Indian Americans, Muslim Americans, Black Americans, etc. America is no longer a confederacy, and although still very active in the political scene at every level of government, it's only a matter of time when diversity will be the authority. So, if it makes the racists feel better by yelling and screaming, calling people Niggers, Sand-Niggers, Chinks and Beaners, then by all means, keep on doing it. If killing Black Americans makes you feel better and you think that this act will somehow improve your way of life in America, think again. Justice will prevail and prison time and lawsuits will become much more common for those murderous terrorists. Confederate politicians and confederate judges and lawyers will soon be a thing of the past within the next 20 years. I feel that there will be no more racist authority in power to pardon and excuse the heinous crimes. A diverse justice system reflecting a diverse America will rise. I would suggest to racists: get used to the new evolving America full of diversity. It would really benefit your children in the long run to learn how to play and get along with diversity rather than trying to teach them to crush diversity. America is no longer a black and white issue if you have not noticed, and no one is going anywhere. End the racism, end the hate and end the NGH ideology!

As far as I am concerned, it's just another NGH moment for poor Mr. Cain. Just like the other black followers of Trump, who would follow this man right into a gas chamber and close the door behind them while Trump exits an escape door at the opposite end! If anyone is familiar with how early classic Hollywood white folks would dress themselves up as other minorities like Asians, Natives and Blacks, by wearing cultural clothing and darkening their faces with make-up, they would know how pathetic it was! I often wonder about those Black Americans at these Trump rallies. Are they actually white folks disguised in Hollywood costumes? If so, Hollywood is amazing! But if these are truly "real" Black Americans for Trump, then once again how pathetic! I wonder how they support the Trump campaign. I am sure they donated money. I imagine if they owned a rope company, they would probably donate rope!

Since the murder of George Floyd, there has been another killing of a black man (Rayshard Brooks) by a cop in Atlanta. Apparently, it was reported that the black man was under the influence and had fallen asleep in a fast-food drive-thru. Upon arrival, the police had Rayshard move his car to a parking stall out of the way as traffic was getting backed up in the drive-thru. After the man parked his car, the police began to conduct a field sobriety test, which showed that he was under the influence. Now let me pause for a second. If the man fell asleep in the drive-thru, one could assume that either the man was extremely tired or he in fact was under the influence. Either way, why would a competent police officer with a potential DUI allow this man to get back into his car to move it into a parking stall? After the sobriety test, and once Rayshard was being cuffed, a struggle ensued. Rayshard managed to take away the officer's taser gun and run away. As the cops gave chase, Rayshard turned to fire the taser gun at the officer. This ultimately cost Rayshard his life as the cop returned fire with his duty weapon. One of the first things that came to my mind was, why did Rayshard take that taser, and why did he run? One of my theories was that perhaps he was fearful of the police due to the current climate of black men being killed by cops over and over again. Perhaps he was thinking with an altered mind-set from being under the influence, thinking that if I let this cop cuff me, he may put me on the ground and choke me out or put his knee in my neck. I felt he was honestly in fear of his life. Not to excuse the man for his actions, but the deadly use of force is what I question. As a Black American, and with the many times that I have been pulled over or stopped by the police, I know that it is often a very nerve-racking and anxious feeling you get that has nothing to do with whether you did something wrong or not, but all to do with what is the mindset of this cop. Is he racist? Will he escalate the encounter? Will he attempt to verbally abuse me? Will he threaten me? Will he try to set me up? Will he beat me up? Will he kill me? All this runs through your head due to prior track records of police brutality and senseless killings. Sometimes you just have the urge to want to run away from the police. It almost feels instinctual!

A guy on Facebook posted this saying, "If you did nothing wrong you have no reason to fear the police". Well, not for black men! In this case, yes, a crime was committed, but that does not cancel out the fear. Another friend of mine who is non- black stated, "Well, he shouldn't have fought with the police or tried to run". My immediate thought to such a comment was that it was insensitive and that the action was justified on the part of the cop. As if Rayshard deserved to die. But I also say, perhaps he was already in fear for his life and felt he would rather try to get away rather than submit himself to yet another execution by a cop of a Black American.

On July 21, 2020, The Office of Civil Rights at The United States Department of Health and Human Services, in response to the COVID-19 pandemic, issued guidance to ensure that receivers of federal financial assistance understand that they must comply with Federal civil right laws and regulations that prohibit discrimination on the basis of race, color and national origin. The guidance was reported as necessary to remind providers that unlawful racial discrimination in healthcare will not be tolerated, as minorities have recently been subjected to longer wait times and rejection of treatment. If systemic racism does not exist in America's healthcare system, then I ask those who believe that it doesn't, why would the US Health Department need to issue the stated guidance? Sounds like there is an issue here. Sounds systemic to me!

A couple of months later, and there's another shooting by a cop of a Black American. Today is August 24, 2020, and "Breaking News" reports that yet another shooting has occurred. As the footage is being played, it shows that the cop is following the unarmed man back to his car, where the man's children are waiting for him. As the man is entering his car, the cop shoots him numerous times in the back. *For what reason this time,* I ask myself! A news reporter immediately states, "We don't know what led up to the shooting." Well, yes, of course you don't! But whatever led up to the incident did not call for a shooting, and there is no justification for it! Maybe the man disobeyed an order or something. Or maybe yet, there seems to be a major trend and uptick with cops shooting down Black Americans, and in my personal belief, these shootings are not isolated. My hunch is that the confederate white supremacists' ideology has made its way back into modern-day policing, the way it used to be. Furthermore, perhaps there is a huge push by these racist white folks attempting to kick off a "race war" that they've been trying to start for generations. Even the infamous Charles Manson tried to start a race war between Black Americans and White Americans. The dumbest and craziest shit ever! How can people preoccupy their minds with this stuff? People don't have anything else better to do, like focusing on how to make America great. Killing people is not part of that solution! Hopefully the FBI is on this one, but homeland terrorism constructed by racist people and groups have always been part of America! I won't hold my breath waiting and thinking that the current authority will be getting rid of homeland-terrorism in America any time soon. It isn't on their "to do" list. Perhaps when the day comes that reflects true diversity in American authority, I would expect that this sort of terrorism would no longer be tolerated here in the United States and that terrorists would be eradicated just like they "eradicate" terrorists in foreign territories. Jacob Blake, the young Black male that was just shot seven times by police, has survived. It is reported that he is out of surgery and in the ICU, paralyzed from the waist down. His mother Julia Jackson stated that there are good cops, but that there are a few bad apples. She is right on with her statement! These bad apples should have never been selected into law enforcement. I guess some law enforcement communities don't mind the lawsuits for a life! Sending prayers to the young man and his family for his survival and speedy recovery.

The young white male from Wisconsin, 17 years old, was allowed to casually walk down the street with an assault rifle. Some say he was there to help prevent looting. However, he wound up killing two innocent people and injuring another. These killings took place in plain view of the police. Multiple police cars were within view as bystanders were recording the killings on their cell phones. The young white male even approached a police vehicle and had a brief conversation with an officer. The shooter is not apprehended as he continues down the street with his assault rifle and later heads back home. I ask myself, did these cops already know that this young man would be there as the reason for their failure to perform their police duties? The assailant is later arrested at his home for the killings. Perhaps the police didn't realize they were caught on cell phone videos and realized they needed to do something about the situation. If not, the young white male may not have been apprehended at all! The protest is over an unarmed Black American shot seven times by a white police officer, and the officer has only been suspended! No arrests have been made and it is now day three since this has taken place. Some people say, "Do not rush to judgment. You do not know what took place before the young Black American was shot seven times in the back". And you see people, this is exactly why groups like BLM exist. A trained police officer knows that in that particular situation, a shooting was in no way warranted nor justified. There is such a thing as a progressive use of force. What that means is that depending on the circumstances of the situation, you start with the least amount of force necessary to deal with a situation. It starts with verbal commands and physical restraints, not choking or a knee to the neck!

Officers know what type of physical force is legal. Deadly force is ONLY to be used when there is an immediate threat of the loss of life to the officer or the life of an innocent citizen. To take things a bit deeper, let's pose a hypothetical situation. Say the young Black American had just killed someone prior to being approached by police. If that young Black American is now unarmed and no longer holds a weapon, the police still cannot shoot that person, as he is no longer a threat. That is why we have a court system! More reports are now coming from the police that the young Jacob Blake was wanted and that he had a knife in his vehicle. Whether he had a knife or a gun in his vehicle, it was not in his hands at the time of the shooting. It is so common for Americans to try and justify the reason an unarmed Black American is gunned down by a police officer.

You hear things like, "Well, he shouldn't have resisted" or "He must have done something," "He was a drug user," "He was a bad person," on and on and on. There is NO justification for the shooting of any unarmed American whatsoever! And the folks who try to justify the shooting of unarmed Black Americans have fallen for the American propaganda campaign and/or are racist. As you can see, there are and always have been two justice systems in America. A system for White Americans and a system for Black Americans, in which whites are given the benefit of the doubt more often than not and are often relieved of crimes they commit, even for the most serious crimes of assault and murder. The Black American is guilty before the facts are laid out and punishment is almost always swift and severe. Especially when compared to the White American. "Disparities in police stops, in prosecutorial charging and in bail and sentencing decisions reveal that implicit racial bias has penetrated all corners of the criminal justice system. Moreover, policies that are race-neutral on their surface-such as "hot spot" policing and certain risk assessment instruments have targeted low-income people of color for heightened surveillance and punishment...people of color are disproportionately punished even for crimes that they do not commit at higher rates than whites" (Ghandnoosh, 2014). This dual justice system can also be found in other aspects of society and not just in the criminal justice system dating back to the 17th century. Systemic racism at its finest!

These continued murders of unarmed Black Americans are terrorist acts! Nothing more, nothing less. White confederacy and supremacy are built on terrorist acts. They scare, intimidate, threaten, torture and kill, all acts which define the meaning of terrorism. These are terrorist groups

POLITICAL REFLECTIONS AND CURRENT HAPPENINGS

right here in America that have been terrorizing and bullying Black Americans ever since the "birth" of this nation. Terrorism is defined in the Code of Federal Regulations as "the unlawful use of force and violence against persons or property to intimidate or coerce a government, the civilian population, or any segment thereof, in furtherance of political or social objectives". A terrorist is, "a person who uses unlawful violence and intimidation, especially against civilians, in the pursuit of political aims". The government is really good at identifying and classifying terrorists and terrorism abroad and even pride themselves on eradicating these terrorist groups in other countries. Isn't it kind of interesting that we can have terrorists going about their daily lives right here in America! The government will point out a foreign terrorist's social media and propaganda tactics and will make note of American-bred terrorist organizations as well. However, all is done to conquer and dismantle foreign terror groups, while nothing seems to be done to conquer and dismantle American bred terror groups!

September 8, 2020, CNN "BREAKING NEWS." Today it is reported that the FBI lists white supremacists as the single most important terror threat to America in the upcoming year of 2021. Why doesn't the American government do something about these American bred terror organizations? If they are reporting about it, then they know about it. I mean, damn, it's okay to seek out and kill foreign terrorists in foreign lands, but they won't even touch or arrest terrorist groups and its members right in its own backyard! But because these inbred terror groups are only out to terrorize and kill blacks and other minority Americans, these groups are no threat to the greater White American community. Therefore, these supremacist terror groups will be left alone to terrorize and kill more innocent lives. I would assume systemic governmental racist politicians will write it off as "freedom of speech". Yet there are those that want to demonize a group such as BLM by calling them "extremists" and "anarchists," when all they want is fair and equal treatment and to stop being terrorized! You see, this is how Black Americans know that their lives don't matter. It's all that we see all around us: contradictions, unfair policies, unfair practices, propaganda, stereotypes. And it just doesn't stop! You can't tell me a black life matters with all the terror that has been afflicted and these terror groups are allowed to continue to plot and remain active in this country. Hypocrisy is alive and well in America, especially when it comes to race relations and self-serving political agendas!

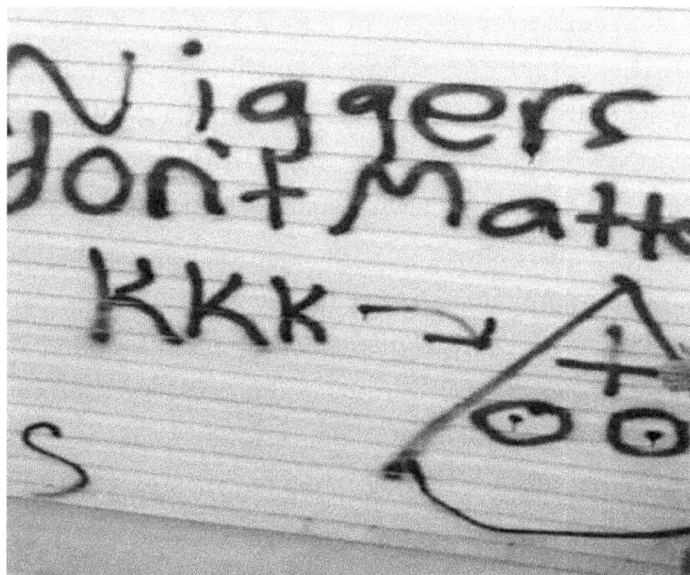

Figure 9 Graffiti 2020 following mass protests around the county.

During the Democratic National Convention on August 19, 2020, former President Obama gave a powerful speech regarding the current state of affairs of America and acknowledged all the reasons why this election year is one of "THE" most important times in history to go out and vote. During his speech, he stated, "GO BACK WHERE YOU CAME FROM." He was referring to all the racists who tell minorities to go back to their countries of origin. Well, this is what these kinds of people have been telling minorities! Muslims, Asians, Middle Easterners, Indians, etc., and this is what they have been telling Black Americans since the abolishment of slavery in the 1800s, "NIGGERS GO HOME!". NGH doesn't have a tangible meaning and it is unrealistic to say the least. NGH is a simile, which means that racist people do not want you in their presence and do not want to interact with you. NGH means they don't want you to participate in American society, become educated, seek employment, vote or obtain wealth. They want to blame you for crime, disease and a bad economy while these same people commit massacres, pass anti- black laws and still continue to instill fear, terrorize and kill. This is what NGH means. Through systemic racism, discrimination and intimidation, NGH is with Black Americans every time they leave their homes. Whether covert or overt, NGH has always been the message given in America and is not exclusive to the Black American!

On October 19, 2020, in the early morning hours, and not far from my home in Sacramento County, a Black American was found hanging from a basketball rim at Countryside Park. The man is named Willie Brown Jr. According to reports, the Sacramento Sheriff's Department has not shared any information with the public and family and have ruled the hanging an apparent suicide. The victim's family and his community believe that Mr. Brown's death is highly suspicious, as there were no signs of evidence of how Mr. Brown could have hung himself from the basketball rim without the use of a ladder or some other object to assist reaching the height of the rim. Hopefully an investigation will be conducted, and the circumstances will become clearer in the pursuit of justice.

As I am reading through my manuscript for the seventh time. It is Saturday November 14, 2020. I received a message from my half-cousin who lives in the Los Angeles area and still has very strong family ties back in Louisiana. She has informed me that a suspicious death has occurred of a 15-year-old black male by the name of Quawan Charles, in the same parish as the Simon Massacre. The young black boy went missing on October 30, 2020, and his body was found on November 3, 2020, in a sugar cane field. Apparently, authorities are ruling it a drowning in the very shallow waters of the sugar cane field and are refusing to investigate the circumstances of the death any further. The family of the young boy stated that he died in a brutal hate crime after being picked up by a white mother and her son, who the parents of the young black boy did not know. It is said that the young boy was picked up from his father's house by the white mother and son duo who refused to speak to the family of Quawan Charles. Prayers and thoughts to the unfortunate loss of life to the family of the murdered boy in Iberia Parish, Louisiana. In 2020, we are still being murdered behind racist ideologies. What a shame!

Black Americans have been put on alert in October about information that white supremacist terrorist groups will be going around kidnapping Black Americans for the purpose of torture and murder. Although the source of these threats is unknown, it was initially reported that the NAACP were the ones to receive information regarding the threats. However, the NAACP has since denied receiving any. With the unusual circumstances surrounding the last two noted incidents, and many more from around the country, it appears that something is going on and with the reluctance of the authorities to investigate these cases any further, it's quite concerning.

My half-cousin further tells me of a recent incident she encountered. She lives in a gated community in Rancho Cucamonga, California. One day a white neighbor with his dog shows up at her front door. Not knowing exactly where the man lives, he tells my cousin to get a bag to clean up his dog's crap off her own front lawn. Now wait… you have a dog and you have the audacity to tell this Black American to get a bag and clean up dog shit from your dog, off her own lawn! She proceeds to curse at him and tells him to get off her property. As the white man is walking away with his dog, he shouts to her, "Fuck you black bitch, black lives don't matter"! As he walked away, he threatened to return to slash her car tires. Needless to say, my cousin took matters into her own hands and returned this man a favor. She was unfortunately arrested on a misdemeanor. This is exactly what I was saying about two systems. This racist man can walk onto your property and harass and intimidate you, but if you as a Black American react, you most likely will be subjected to some form of penalty or punishment. These folks will try to incite you, they will come up in your face, call you a NIGGER, call you a bitch and whatever else to get you to snap so they can toss you into jail. Black Americans, be careful of not only racial attacks and white terrorism, be aware of the set-up!

Figure 10 Graffiti 2020 following mass protests around the county.

WHO ARE WE?

Without roots, I have struggled through the years trying to identify with who I am and who my people are. As a young boy growing up, I recall a time when most Black Americans (mostly the adults) would pass each other by and would respectfully acknowledge one another by a nod of the head or "How's it going?". I recall that if a conversation ensued, one of the first questions the adults would ask one another was, "where are your people from?" I felt that this type of commonality was a sense of solidarity, a way Black Americans offered each other a bit of support, as a way of saying, "You're not alone in this strange and hostile country".

I'm often envious of other ethnic cultures as they partake and celebrate in ceremonious activities, including their display of arts and their exotic foods. I get why Black Americans are conflicted with what or how they want to be identified here in America. I get why there are many that would rather be referred to as African American rather than Negro or

Black. It gives one a sense of belonging, belonging to a foundation that traces back to ancient times and reflecting direct lineage. It is what makes us human. Unfortunately, cloudiness, murkiness and darkness from the 17th century (around 1619) until 1865, has brought an endless dark eclipse and an unintentional forgetfulness of one's native home and cultures. Despite being intentional amongst anti-abolitionists, we were existent but non-existent. When this eclipse passed, Black Americans had to re-create themselves. America is the birthplace of the Black American, whose descendants before them experienced long sea voyages, illnesses, death, bondage, beatings, terrorism and broken families. Descendants who produced offspring would pass down life skills needed for survival, while contributing to the abandonment of free nature, of free culture, of free life, now living on natural instinct and the natural human response to live, thrive, and survive. Descendants in a new world who were surrounded and dominated by entities outside themselves, motivated by a passion to use, eliminate and then destroy in a similar fashion to the movement to stamp-out, eliminate and destroy the Natives of America for selfish gains and greediest passions. So here we are!

We are not what they tell us we are! I will not let the media dictate who I am. Do not let the media dictate who you are!

Since slavery, American media (or racist media to be more accurate), has depicted Black America to fit their agendas based out of white greed, white fear and white hate. They want America to see Black Americans as hoodlums, drug dealers, pimps, out-laws, dysfunctional, uneducated, rapists, murderers, promiscuous, immoral, thieves, savages, animals, predators, and unintelligent with lazy and complacent minds. The non-thinkers are easily manipulated and will accept these as the only complete truths. What is even more unfortunate is Black Americans who play right into these framed stereotypes as if to follow the pied piper right into the web of the Jim Crows, racists laws and judicial systems. The racist American media would prefer ALL to believe that Black Americans are what they say we are. But I know better and many of us know better. We know who we are! We are survivalists, strategists, scientists, artists, lawyers, judges, doctors, church leaders, social providers, nurses, inventors, accomplishers, performers, scholars, construction workers, politicians, managers, educators, activists, authors, mechanics, and the list goes on. Existing in a pool of adversities within Black American life, these adversities have been stacked high. For some, too high. Milestones have taken too long, and amidst the long journey in search of freedom and equality, Black America still persists. They persevered through slavery, through segregation, through stereotypes, assumptions, labels, discrimination, systemic racism, through medical experimentation and through hundreds of years of terrorism. Black America continues to survive, continues to thrive and is still seeking to be free. Free to live without harassment, free to live without judgment and prejudice, free to live anywhere, and most importantly, free to live without fear. Like the fear from being gunned down by a terroristic racist police officer or hung by a terroristic white supremacist. I would undoubtedly have to say that Black America is triumphant in survival and remains steadfast in being recognized as positive contributing members of American society regardless of any and all attempts meant to destroy us!

WHO ARE YOU?

Are you for a better America? Are you for a racist free America? Do you know those with strong racist views and perceptions? Do you accept those views and perceptions? Do you deny people's factual accounts? Do you accept news at face value? Do you fact check what you are told or taught? Do you believe everything in the media? Do you follow and stand with the masses, or do you stand up for what is right? Do you stand up for morality? Do you stand up against terror? Are you for equality? Are you for fairness? Do you judge people by the way they look, or do you get to know their character? Do you hold assumptions? Do you believe in the future? Do you believe in a higher creator? Do you believe in division? Do you believe in separatism? Lastly, are you for a UNITED States? If so, these are the things one must ask themselves and those of the people they know. Reflect on these questions, and you may learn a lot about yourself. For some, these questions will also help you to figure out where you stand on race relations in America.

Identifying your core beliefs and being honest with yourself will help to shift the culture of race relations in America for the positive, through new attitudes and a new desire to shape the attitudes and opinions of future generations.

It doesn't take a government official or someone with credentials to put you in a box and label you as this or that. You do not have to identify with being a Democrat or a Republican or a right-wing or a left-wing. Human beings are way more complex than that. You can be conservative when it comes to some things and totally liberal when it comes to others. You are how you see the world around you and how you live your life and envision the lives of your children and grandchildren for future generations. We all want the best for our children, not just Whites, not just Blacks, not just Hispanics, not just Asians. Each and every one of us wants what is best for our children. That is a universal fact. It starts with teaching and showing the younger generations how to respect one another, so the focus is no longer on race relations but on environmental and global well-being. All humans have the right to freedom, and no one should be above or below the law. So, who are you, and what kind of country do you want to leave behind for your children? One that is divided or one that is united?

CONCLUSION

Some people that you share your life experiences with will sometimes have strong opinions when it comes to Black Americans and racism. Some whites and other non-black minorities often will debate you when it comes to the Black American and their daily stories of living in a racist society. Many times, the comment of "the race card" comes out or that you're "over-analyzing" and even being "hyper-sensitive". Many doubters downplay or even outright reject your experiences! What perplexes me is how one can speak on your personal life and tell you how to interpret your experience, as if you are too dumb to articulate it yourself. This is where Black Americans get frustrated! We know our experiences better than anyone on the outside looking in, and although other Black Americans can relate, they still do not know your personal experience 100%. When we share our stories and you do not agree with what we share with you, then it would be polite of you not to re-create or debate. When you do that, you come off as lacking empathy and compassion, being insensitive and "almost" sounding racist. Keep an open ear and an open mind but save your surprised reactions and your doubting looks for a different subject. Black Americans are sensitive to this, and unless you take us seriously, then the feeling we are often left with is despair and that the greater community will never understand Black Life in America. America, if you really want to get serious about ending and eradicating racism, you need to focus on inclusion for ALL!

Start by acknowledging that racism is real. Then get rid of those racial ethnicity checkboxes on applications for jobs, school admissions, loan and credit documents and everywhere else where race should not matter. These boxes are ridiculously outdated and not needed. They are only meant to screen out rather than include. It plays a big part in the foundation of systemic racism. Schools should teach K-12 students about racial tolerance, teach diversity, teach the truth in American history, acknowledge the cruel and inhumane treatment of slaves and indigenous people, teach how not to hate and promote a respectful environment for all. Unfortunately, there are many adults and parents that do nothing but teach and pass down hate, so it must be left up to the schools to try and counter the racist beliefs and attitudes.

With the recent issues regarding defacing and removing historical statues and monuments, I think this was one of the most unintelligent things this country could have allowed. Of course, many statues are of confederate, racist murderers and terrorists of past leaders who bring back harsh and painful memories. However, I believe they should have left those alone as it is part of American history! Why do you think we didn't get the truth of American history in grade school? Because they want to omit it and act like nothing bad ever took place in this country. So now folks want to omit this truth! Keep the statues up and ensure that the truth is displayed alongside those statues. Include information like how many slaves they kept or how many slaves they killed or how many peaceful protesters and voters were beaten and tortured. And to take things even further, put up more statues of ethnic folks such as Asian Americans, Native Americans, Black Americans, Mexican and Latin Americans and all Americans of color who have made some positive significance and contribution to this country. Let America reflect in its statues people of all backgrounds and all colors as equally as white statues so that we can begin to become a UNITED States.

I said earlier how people don't listen to Black Americans and their stories. Well, what really gets me is when someone will tell you, "If you don't like it here, why don't you move to another country". If that's not a classic NGH statement! People who agree with such an insensitive statement come off extremely ignorant. Africans arrived in the

United States of America once colonization began. Those first Africans who arrived here with those first Europeans were not native to America, nor were the Europeans. The Native Americans were, but as we all know, that is another tragic story at the hands of colonizing Europeans. African slaves are responsible for the wealth of America (cotton was worth more than oil), and it wasn't Europeans harvesting cotton! Exploited by Europeans through enslavement and forced labor, America was built on the backs of Black Americans through all sorts of hard labor. Yet who did that benefit? The ones with the guns and sick sadistic mindsets! So, why NGH? America was never the Europeans' homeland in the first place. The most ridiculous statement I have ever heard! Honestly, it should be the RACISTS who don't like it here and that have issues with Blacks, Asians, Hispanics, Middle Easterners, etc. that should go! Perhaps Racist Confederates Go Home or RCGH! America is meant to be and destined to be United, not divided! How can this country ever be united when folks think the solution for people who have legitimate complaints should leave? Racist people are not wanted in America. Minorities and other intelligent White citizens want to progress this nation with intellectual candor, seeking out solutions together amongst all citizens for combating disease, addressing climate change and advancing in technology. We want a smart, inclusive America, not a dumbed-down racist America reflective of 19th and

20th century practices. The people want a 21st-century logical political system that is fair to every citizen in America. The majority of people in America want to set an example to the rest of the world to show that people from all diversities can live united and in harmony. Racism and terrorism in America are a distraction to the greater potential of this country and it is amazing that this country as a whole tolerates natural-born terrorism. If America is ready to make this a United and Great country, then it must eradicate its terrorists!

Another thing America can do to help build its greatness is to stop hiring so many insensitive police officers who are hungry to brutalize Black Americans! It starts with the selection process prior to the academy. Does every police agency run extensive background checks? If not, this should be a top priority. Perhaps if they did, they would learn through a background check that an applicants' social media posts or the social media of their associates reveal that the soon to be officer is affiliated with a terrorist organization such as a white supremacy group. Perhaps another cop killing an unarmed Black American could be avoided. It seems like police departments throughout this country are okay with being sued behind racist cops. Perhaps start recruiting more officers to patrol the towns and cities in which they live. So many cops come down from the hills, come out of the suburbs to patrol black and ethnic neighborhoods. Do they understand the culture? Do they get cultural sensitivity training? I am sure many come in filled with media stereotypes ready to regulate with unnecessary force! Policing should be carried out by at least 90 percent of those from their own communities. Another idea would be to ban pulling people over for minor infractions. We are living in a world so technically advanced that there should be no reason for a police officer to make a stop on every traffic violation. If a red light was run, snap the picture. If a taillight is busted, snap a picture. If a registration has expired, snap a picture. There should be no reason why police officers are stopping citizens for minor violations unless they are in pursuit or on call of a legitimate felony violation. End racial profiling and insist that police officers must ensure every stop of a person can articulately be justified by that officer. If the justification cannot be legitimized, then the officer should be subjected to some form of disciplinary action.

Here is another idea: Since there seem to be two justice systems (one for White Americans and one for Black Americans), and White Americans run both systems, if this society wants to continue with that status quo, then Black Americans should have their own justice system. We do not need permission, as permission wasn't given to those afflicted by historic and current injustices brought against Black America. Why do we look to those who oppress us to write the rules and laws that we all abide by like herded sheep?

How about Black Americans create their own rules and policies governing their lives in society? Very much like what already exists, but without the oversight of a systemic racist leadership with confederate, Jim Crow and discriminative ideologies and practices. Why does such a racist system have so much power and influence over the people they oppress? Perhaps a separate justice system will bring those American bred terrorists to justice since the current one has proven incapable. This is an idea, one I would not support. I support diversity and I truly believe that in the next couple of decades American power will gradually begin to look more and more diverse.

Another idea to help rid out systemic racism is by creating a racial rating system. Let's call it the RRS. A system that rates businesses according to how they treat and interact with their minority customers. This country has become so obsessed with ratings for things like movies, restaurants, businesses, etc. This should also be accomplished in rating racist encounters in American social and business structures. If a company or business has bad ratings with minority relations, then all minorities and supportive White Americans shall avoid and stop doing business with these companies. Rating systems should also be implemented in police departments. For departments that have less than good ratings, then those police departments should be subjected to less funding as well as disciplinary actions taken against officers who contribute to the low ratings.

The census data is done every ten years and is used to help make decisions, such as where to send needed resources, new schools, new roads and highways, new businesses, emergency services and where populations have increased or decreased. Hesitant to complete the survey, I started to fill it out just to see the types of questions they would be asking. They want to know if you are of Hispanic, Latino, Spanish origin, White, Black, American Indian, Alaskan Native, Chinese, Korean, Filipino or another Asian race and ethnicity. My question is, if we are all here legally in America, then why do people need to identify their ethnic origins and racial identities? Aren't we all Americans? If the government needs to figure out where resources are needed, I am sure they already know where resources are needed. How about the political decision-makers taking a drive around the communities and towns they oversee? You already know what and where resources are needed. With all this technology, you mean to tell me they need a census survey to figure out where to send resources? These political leaders drive these highways, freeways and roads every day, and not only that, I am sure they get reports on damaged infrastructure. Hell, you can use satellite technology to see what is needed! If you can see a damn rock on Mars and analyze its composition, then I am pretty confident you can see a crack on an aging bridge or infrastructure. Isn't that what constituents are for, to let top leaders know what is needed in their jurisdictions? And the public is told that it is important to complete this census data survey, or they will lose out! Please, arrest the manipulation and free the transparency!

Black American and minority communities have been losing out despite any prior census data surveys. In a racist run society, low-income neighborhoods will always be the last to get any new resources. So, forget it, I am not filling out this stupid census shit. There is another agenda behind it, and I am not falling for it. We currently live in a racist system and I am convinced the census data is used to ensure resources don't go where they are most needed. Pops would always point out how the grocery stores in the poorest neighborhoods got less quality produce and meats than the more affluent neighborhoods. I have gone grocery shopping in poor areas and in more affluent neighborhoods, and yep, he was right! Once the racist attacks stop, once discrimination stops, once equality is achieved and proven in this country, then it makes no damn sense to complete a census data survey. I've been lied to on surveys before, I'm good!

Eradicating racism in this country can be accomplished. I have faith in this country. There are very good and sincere Americans who mean well, work hard and truly have good hearts. Racist people and the old confederate way of thinking are a minority in this country. The problem is that this minority has been the majority voice in politics, business and education for generations. This ideology will one day fizzle out and hopefully, sooner than later, America can begin healing and be united, becoming great just like the majority of unheard voices so desperately desire.

Finally, I wrote this book to acknowledge my truth and the American truth regarding race relations, in a quest for healing to take place in a country that has been so divided by race for so long. I have hope that this country will one day be born again, born free of hate, racism and prejudice into a country where all people from all ethnic backgrounds are treated equally and not judged by their appearances. Free to live in the pursuit of happiness and to obtain fulfilled dreams. Without understanding and learning the truth about the past or forgetting the past and omitting the past, we will most definitely and ultimately watch our society repeat the past. Opening up the mind with an inclusive attitude for all, while understanding differences, sharing those differences and respecting those differences, is what will make America great. America is at a point where it can no longer tolerate racism, prejudice and hate, and if Americans can't agree on this, then America is bound for a collision course in meeting its fate.

With this year's United States Presidential election, I decided to wait to publish this book until November for the turn-out of the election. The race for presidency is between the current President Donald Trump and former Vice President Mr. Joe Biden. He served as Vice President alongside Barack Obama, the first President of color with a heritage of African roots, from 2009 to 2017. Knowing that this is a major election, and the most important election year of American history, this book would not be complete without recording the results of the election. The atmosphere in America has been toxic and Americans have been sitting on edge wondering how much more toxicity it can bear. The virus of hate seems to be at an all-time high. America now leads the world in the number of cases and deaths regarding the COVID-19 virus. Americans are tired and weary and seek hope for the future. It is November 7, 2020, as I wake up to a brisk cool morning. I converge to my spot to begin my morning ritual of 30 minutes of stretching and listening to the news. As I am listening, the "Breaking News" report is that Mr. Joe Biden has been declared victorious for President elect! Hallelujah! As I thank God, chills run throughout my body as I know immediately that positive change is on its way for this country. For so many reasons this seems even bigger than Mr. Barack Obama becoming the first Black American President. With so much on the line in this country, America cannot afford another four years of a directionless, wannabe dictator running the current administration.

But why Mr. Joe Biden? He is a white man! Here is the answer: it doesn't matter what race, creed, nationality or gender you are, as long as you represent ALL America. He is inclusive and concerned about ALL people and is for the people! Taking progress even further, Mr. Biden has selected a woman of color, Ms. Kamala Harris as his VP! She comes from African and Indian/Asian descent and is from my hometown of the Bay Area! How impressive is that! Not only the first woman ever to become Vice President in America, but the first woman of color! As I mentioned before, America needs to be healed, healed from racist and confederate ideology and healed from the COVID-19 virus. Mr. Joe Biden and Senator Kamala Harris give us a new hope by bringing in their wealth of experience and their desire to serve all American citizens (even the racist ones), in creating a fair and UNITED nation. Their election is necessary to bring this country around from its not-so-great past, to making America great for everyone! The majority of America is overzealous. As we recognize that positive and united change is on the horizon, the excitement runs deep while Americans all over are celebrating peacefully in the streets! The reflection of the crowds in celebration are a reflection of the multicultural depth of this country. It feels good! It feels like and looks like a UNITED America and most importantly it feels like HOME! America's history of NGH and its ideology will soon fade away within the next few generations and will only be recognized as a memory and learned about in future generational academic studies. However, it seems that Trump is not going out without a fight, claiming the election was a rigged process. It feels as though this country is under siege, and that Trump is not for the American people. He seems to be the Enemy of States. He is a puppet to the enemies of this country and that is why we have so much uncertainty and death plaguing America right now. Let's hope we survive the last months with this man in office!

Mr. Joe Biden, the President elect, stated the first deal of business is putting together a strategic plan and creating a team to get a hold of the COVID-19 virus. This is the first time, since the virus has plagued America, that a plan will be the top priority of the new Administration. There has been no plan, other than to allow thousands of Americans to be infected and ultimately die. I must say that it is truly a moment of celebration! There is a lot of healing that lies ahead for America. Mr. Joe Biden stated that "This is the time to heal in America", which is so important and necessary for the overall health and well-being of the country. He also mentioned that America can do and accomplish anything as a United country and eradicating hate is part of that healing. The Americans who seek division, separatism and exclusion of a multicultural nation will soon be a thing of the past. It would be a benefit to your children and your grandchildren to teach them how to play and get along with others without judgment based on appearances. That simple-minded destructive nature is no longer tolerated in this country as reflected by the outcome of the 2020 presidential election. America is no longer a white and black issue, as diversity is now the majority. From here on out, America will only become more and more diverse. The demographics have changed and continue to change, and that change is diverse people of mixed ethnic backgrounds who continue to multiply. Hopefully one day, ethnicity check boxes on employment applications, loan applications, census data, etc. will be a thing of the past. It is not necessary to try and identify one's ethnicity in a truly free and equal country. Let's end hate and become, for the first time, a truly UNITED States. Anything can be accomplished in America!

Figure 11, 1800s-Mary Ned, Great, Great Grandmother, and former Slave.

BIBLIOGRAPHY

Anti-Defamation League. (2020). Reports of Anti-Asian Assaults, Harassment and Hate Crime Rise. ADL.

Boissoneault, L. (2018). The 1873 Colfax Massacre Crippled the Reconstruction Era. Smithsonian Magazine/Smart News.

Boissoneault, L. (2018). The 1873 Colfax Massacre Crippled the Reconstruction Era. Smithsonian Magazine.

Boissoneault, L. (2018). The 1873 Colfax Massacre Crippled the Reconstruction Era. Smithsonian Magazine; Equal Justice Initiative.

Boissoneault, L. (2018). The Deadliest Massacre in Reconstruction- Era Louisiana Happened 150 Years Ago. Smithsonian Magazine.

Boskin, L. G. (1986). Sambo: The Rise & Demise of an American Jester. New York: Oxford University Press.

Brewster, M. L. (2015). What's Behind Racial Differences in Restaurant Tipping. The Washington Post.

Cedars, C. M. (2014). Letter from Birmingham Jail Bibliography. GradeSaver.

Chokshie, N. (2018). Racism at American Pools Isn't New: A Look at a Long History. New York Times.

Costello/Douez. (2017). Segregation in Public Places/ Remembering Jim Crow. American Public Media.

Dearman, E. (2020). El Paso Reflects on Racist Motive behind August 3rd Walmart Mass Shooting. El Paso Times.

Douez, D., & Costello, E. (2017). Roots of Racism: 6 essential reads. The Conversation.

Du Bois, W. (1928). The Name "Negro"-Teaching American History.

Eli Moore, N. M. (2019). Roots, Race, & Place: A History of Racially Exclusionary Housing in the San Francisco Bay Area. Haas Institute, University of California, Berkeley.

Frakt, A. (2020). The Harm That Comes from Mistrust. New York Times.

Gambhir, S. M. (2019). Racial Segregation in the San Francisco Bay Area. Othering & Belonging Institute; Part 2, Publication.

Jordan, W. D. (1968). White Over Black, American Attitudes Towards the Negro, 1550-1812. The University of North Carolina Press, Chapel Hill.

Kendall, M. (2019). For Whites Only: Shocking Language Found in Property Docs Throughout Bay Area. The Mercury News, Media News Group, Inc., 2020.

Lawrence, A. (2018). How the "Natural Talent" myth is used as a Weapon Against Black Athletes. The Guardian.

Long, H. (2017). Democracy Dies in Darkness. The Washington Post.

Martin, B. L. (1991). From Negro to Black to African American: The Power of Names and Naming. Political Science Quarterly.

Ph.D., N. G. (2014). Race and Punishment: Perceptions of Crime and Support for Punitive Policies. The Sentencing Project.

Speri, A. (2019). The FBI and Its Fictional "Black Identity Extremism" Movement; Fear of a Black Homeland. The Intercept.

Streeter, L. a. (2016). Black Activists Don't Ignore Crime. The New York Times.

The New Orleans. (1888).

The New York Times. (1888). Surrendering Their Arms; Matters About Freetown Resuming Their Normal Condition. The New York Times.

The Opportunity Agenda. (2004). Media Portrayals and Black Male Outcomes. Center for Media and Public Affairs.

Thernstrom, A. a. (1998). Black Progress. Brookings.

W.E.B. Du Bois (1928) The Name "Negro" - Teaching American History.

Wilson, V. (2019). Economic Policy Institute.

Wiltse, J. (2010). Swimming in the Long Shadows of Segregation. St. Louis Post-Dispatch.

Wright, M. W. (2016). North Carolina cop: This Fear of Black Men is Real. The Undefeated.

www.ingramcontent.com/pod-product-compliance
Lightning Source LLC
Chambersburg PA
CBHW060231050426

42448CB00009B/1386